the

MORAL

center

ALSO BY DAVID CALLAHAN

The Cheating Culture:
Why More Americans Are Doing
Wrong to Get Ahead

DAVID CALLAHAN

the
MORAL
center

How We Can Reclaim Our Country from
Die-Hard Extremists, Rogue Corporations,
Hollywood Hacks, and Pretend Patriots

HARCOURT, INC.

ORLANDO   AUSTIN   NEW YORK   SAN DIEGO   TORONTO   LONDON

www.HarcourtBooks.com

Library of Congress Cataloging-in-Publication Data
Callahan, David, 1965–
The moral center: how we can reclaim our country from die-hard extremists, rogue
corporations, Hollywood hacks, and pretend patriots/David Callahan.—1st ed.
p.   cm.
1. Social values—United States.   2. Self-interest—United States.   3. Social problems—
United States.   4. United States—Moral conditions.   5. Liberalism—United States.
6. Conservatism—United States.   7. Right and left (Political science).   I. Title.
HN90.M6C35   2006
303.3'720973—dc22   2006008292
ISBN-13: 978-0-15-101151-3   ISBN-10: 0-15-101151-6

Text set in Adobe Jensen
Designed by Cathy Riggs

Printed in the United States of America
First edition
A C E G I K J H F D B

For my parents, Daniel and Sidney Callahan,
who shaped my values

And for my wife, Wendy Paris,
who helps me live them

contents

preface

Back in the late 1990s I helped start a think tank, Demos, which hoped to tell a new story about how to make America a better place. We set up shop during the dotcom madness, and sometimes—especially when I read the business page every morning—I wondered whether the age of ideas and politics had passed. It often seemed that the real action lay elsewhere and that if I really wanted to affect how people lived I should join a technology company or a venture capital firm, or get hip to various synergies in the media world.

I didn't do any of these things. And, as Demos took form, one of our themes was that Americans shouldn't leave their destiny in the hands of private market actors who were growing more powerful. Instead, we thought that people should come together to protect the human values we shared.

The go-go 1990s are long gone and we now live in a time when nobody can doubt the importance of politics or ideology. At the same time, market forces have only gotten stronger. Every day I see more evidence that we can't take for granted such basic values as time for family, a fair reward for hard work, our obligations to protect each other from misfortune, and our ability to shape the beliefs of our own children.

This is a short book on a very big topic. I do not try to cover everything and there are many issues left unaddressed. In particular, I don't delve deeply into religion and its role in our society—not because faith isn't central to any understanding of values in the United States, a point I make often in the pages ahead, but rather because there are so many others who have written extensively in this area. Likewise, if you're looking for detailed policy solutions, you've come to the wrong place. While I do offer many prescriptions to address the problems discussed in each chapter, I do not include in-depth explanations of how these policies would work. My goal with this book is to advance a different way of thinking about values, along with promising ideas for changing America, not to provide a comprehensive blueprint for action.

I am grateful to various people who helped me develop my thinking and make this book possible. Over these last years Demos has provided me with a home and colleagues, with whom I have enjoyed extended conversation about many of arguments in this book. I'm grateful to Charlie Halpern and Stephen Heintz who were instrumental in creating Demos, as well as to Miles Rapoport, who has so effectively led and built the organization since 2001. I'm also grateful to Tamara Draut for helping me think through my ideas about work and opportunity, and for reading this book in draft form. Many others provided feedback on all or some of the book, including Craig Charney, Jessie Klein, David Smith, and John Schwarz. In researching the book, I conducted many interviews around the country, often with people who see the world very differently than I do. Yet everyone I talked to was helpful, kind, and forthcoming. My thanks to all of them. My editor at Harcourt, Andrea Schulz, has brought pure genius to the challenge of shaping the project, just as she did with my last book. My agent, Andrew Stuart, has been an invaluable friend and a staunch ally, intellectually and professionally.

Finally, I want to thank my wife, Wendy Paris, who has helped me not only to become a better writer and thinker, but also a better person.

CHAPTER ONE

What's Really Wrong

YOU DON'T NEED TO BE A BUSH VOTER OR AN EVAN-
gelical Christian to be worried about the moral climate of America. You don't need to be upset by
abortion or gay marriage or sex ed teachers putting con-
doms on bananas. You don't have to be up in arms about
the influence of Charles Darwin in our schools or the absence of the Ten Commandments from our courthouses.

You may have none of these concerns—and yet still
feel that something is deeply wrong with the values of
America. Maybe you worry that most strangers can't be
trusted. Or that young Americans have lost any sense of
purpose beyond getting rich and famous. Or that Hollywood and Madison Avenue influence children more than
Mom and Dad. Or that millions lack health care in the
world's richest country. Or that having a strong marriage

and family is ever less compatible with making a living. Maybe you gaped at the television images of people stranded in New Orleans and wondered, "How did we ever become so cold-hearted?" Maybe your specific concerns keep changing, but you can't shake the feeling that American life is getting meaner and more degraded, and that everyone is out for themselves.

For me, it's all this and also something else: a sense of constantly being tugged away from my real values. I never cared much about money and never saw myself as a covetous kind of person until I moved to New York City, where I had to walk past the townhouses of the rich every day and started reading magazines like *New York* and the real-estate section of the *New York Times*. With inequality now at levels that rival the Gilded Age, envy may be the most powerful emotional current in America today, and it's hard not to get caught in its grip. We live in a time when so many of us look anxiously upward at what we might have or who we could be, as opposed to looking downward and being thankful for all that has come our way. I consider myself a compassionate person who cares about the misfortunes of others, but I've learned to tune out the beggars on the subway, even the women who tug their children along and tell horrific stories of lost housing or benefits that I know reflect reality. I'm committed to marriage and family—this is the foundation of true meaning and happiness, I understand—but much of the time I put career first, scrambling after an endless series of external rewards. I want to know my neighbors better and get involved in my community, but I'm busy and preoccupied. Maybe next year. It's easy to feel that things are not only getting worse, they are also making you a worse person. I don't have children yet, but I can imagine how parents might lack confidence about passing along their values in this environment.

You're not alone if you share these feelings. While the complaints of the Christian right echo through our politics every day, the truth is that Americans of all political stripes worry about values, in one way or another. This has been obvious for some time. The 1990s were a decade of peace and prosperity—and of Columbine, Monica Lewinsky, and Ferrari-driving twenty-eight-year-old millionaires. Moral angst burned hot beneath the façade of good times, so much so that in 2000 a major poll found that only 12 percent of Americans were satisfied with the moral values of this country, the lowest level for any major issue. More recently, a 2005 poll—echoing other polls—found that a strong majority of Americans believe that people aren't as honest or moral as they used to be, and an even higher percentage see young people as having a weaker sense of right and wrong than they did fifty years ago. Most Americans also feel that we are too tolerant of bad behavior.[1]

It's not that values matter more than other issues. They don't. Scholars like Jeffrey Stonecash and Larry Bartels have documented the enduring—in fact, growing—role of class in politics. Poorer whites in particular are still more focused on economic issues than on social ones, contrary to what Thomas Frank argued in *What's the Matter with Kansas?* But there is also no question that moral concerns have become bigger issues in recent decades and that public anxieties go well beyond the agenda of religious conservatives.[2]

Yes, voters who named "moral values" as their top issue went overwhelmingly for Bush in 2004, and yes, abortion and same-sex marriage have reshaped the political landscape in certain parts of the country. But other issues matter, too. In a Zogby poll conducted after the 2004 election, 33 percent of voters said the nation's biggest moral problem was "greed and materialism" and 31 percent cited "poverty and economic justice." Another post-election survey—of Catholics voters—found that these Americans were more likely to emphasize issues of integrity or the "social compact" when they thought of moral values than to focus on abortion or gay marriage. Earlier polls found that a majority of Americans defined poor health care, as well as inequality between whites and minorities, as moral issues.[3]

These anxieties help explain why values stay on the national agenda despite a steady stream of good news. Violent crime is now down to where it was in the late 1960s.

Abortions declined sharply in the 1990s, reaching the lowest level since 1975. Teen pregnancy rates also plunged dramatically. Births to unwed mothers have stopped rising. Divorce rates have fallen since their high in the late 1970s, particularly among college-educated couples.

Usually when things get better, public debate moves on to other matters. Not this time. And that suggests that the new moral politics is fueled by more than the longstanding concerns of the Christian right. Something bigger is happening.

If you talk across ideological divides—to Americans left, right, and center—a unifying theme of much moral anxiety is a feeling that selfishness is careening out of control. You see this feeling in conservative concerns about divorce—and in liberal anger about corporate crime. You see it in the anti-abortion activism on the right—and in the living wage movement on the left. Conservatives worry that kids today grow up wanting to be porn stars; liberals fear that they want to be investment bankers. A lot of Americans fear that the pursuit of self-interest is pushing aside other values in every aspect of life: family, sex, culture, business, education.

But if people of all stripes worry about selfishness, it is conservatives who have defined what kind of selfishness is wrong, who is to blame for it, and how we can find a better moral compass. The right blames selfishness on liberalism, blasting the hedonism and focus on personal rights that emerged in the 1960s. Their solution to our moral state is simple: America needs to return to religion and traditional values.

You needn't agree with the right on the specifics to find reassurance in such appeals. Whatever you may think about Christian conservatives, at least they offer a plan to get America on a different moral path. At least they clearly say that something has gone very wrong with our moral life. So does the Republican Party that these activists have reshaped in recent decades. And it is no wonder that this party does so well with married voters and parents. Just the fact that conservatives believe it's possible to change the culture may be enough to turn a great many people into GOP "values voters."

The catch is that the moralists on the right don't have a real solution to rising selfishness. Not only have they defined the problem far too narrowly—obsessing about sex especially—they refuse to confront the force that increasingly fans an extreme ethos of self-interest, namely our free-market economy.

THE IDEA THAT market forces are a decisive shaper of values is neither radical nor new. The sociologist Daniel Bell made this argument in his 1976 book *The Cultural Contradictions of Capitalism*. Others had made the point before him, and others have made it since. Strangely, though, even as history has accelerated in recent decades, with globalization and technological change moving at a dizzying pace, this elementary insight into moral life stands largely forgotten. We talk about how "the world is flat" or how this invention or that is altering our daily existence, but we're not so good at connecting these conversations to the values debate.

Capitalism forms the backbone of the American idea that everyone can chart their own destiny and the market fosters so much that is positive. A free market, existing independent of church or state, has long been recognized as a linchpin to personal liberty. Certainly no one has figured out a better way to produce wealth, and it is capitalism that has made America the richest, most dynamic country on earth. Market prosperity has underwritten fantastic leaps forward in our education levels, standard of living, and longevity—all positive moral outcomes. Capitalism can foster other moral results, too: by pushing people to be self-disciplined, by elevating those who work the hardest, by replacing cronyism with competition, and by rewarding people based on their creativity and talent.

But there are obvious moral risks to this system, because it revolves around the pursuit of self-interest. To make the system work and keep the riches flowing, we fan a set of very productive—yet very dangerous—human impulses. We ride the tiger of selfishness. Untamed, it will eat everything we care about. The logic of self-interest can not only go too far in the business realm, as we well know;

its excesses can lap over into other parts of society, such as family, sex, and popular culture. This danger exists in any nation, but it is particularly acute here, where individualism has always been very strong.

Conservatives are in deep denial about this connection. For forty years they have pushed freer markets in concert with a call for stronger moral checks rooted in religion. And for forty years, evidence has piled up that traditionalist values are no match for unfettered capitalism—which among other things has forced parents to work longer hours and given us a multibillion-dollar pornography industry. Of course, you didn't have to live through recent history to know that markets and traditional values don't get along so well. That has been clear ever since mothers and children were sent to toil in nineteenth-century mills and early mass media weakened the influence of religious leaders.

Do conservatives ever seem to learn this basic lesson? Strangely not, and the religious "family values" crowd remains in a tight alliance with pro-business libertarians.

LIBERALS ARE NAÏVE about capitalism in their own way. The left has long promoted an expansive form of individualism—especially since the 1960s. Liberals have said that you should be able to control your own life when it comes to sex, marriage, worship, and other matters. These freedoms were never meant to stand alone; the left championed more personal autonomy and more social responsibility in the same breath. You could do your own thing, sure, but you also were supposed to make the world a better place. The problem is that it's easy to forget about the second half of the equation in a consumer society, especially when—amid a backlash to the 1960s—we were told that earnest idealism was for fools. Ironically, the new individualism of the counterculture helped set the stage for the me-first materialism of the 1980s and '90s.

In a strange way, religious traditionalists and liberal idealists are now in the same boat. Both are increasingly powerless to shape the culture. None of the restraints on moral behavior imagined by left or right have succeeded in an age of turbo-charged global capitalism. Today, it is private actors—developers, corporations, entertainment conglomerates, advertising firms, technology companies—who often determine how people live, and more important, *what they value*. In general, these actors increase their bottom line by fanning our impulses toward personal gratification and individual autonomy. They work at odds with such quaint notions as self-restraint and duty to others. As they have become more dominant, they have come to wield more influence in many cases than the various institutions that once promoted selfless values, such as family, community, religion, and government. And it is not just that market actors have more power. It is that the ethos of the market— the notion that self-interest is the best organizing basis of society—has reordered our moral universe. As a result, it has become easier to rationalize a wide range of selfish behaviors.

This is a big shift, and yet it mostly goes ignored. Even as the idealism of the left and traditionalism of the right are pushed aside by the same bulldozer, both sides still act as if the real moral powerbrokers are federal judges or Congressional firebrands or megachurch ministers. Conservatives write an endless stream of diatribes that trace all of America's moral problems back to Gloria Steinem or the Warren Court, while liberals increasingly define the Christian right as the enemy. This debate misses a dominant fact of our time: Whether you're a moralist on the left or the right, it's hard to practice your values in a society that has become mostly about self-interest.

These days it's easy to get caught up in "culture war" talk. And make no mistake: The polarization between traditionalists and modernists is real. But there is another rift in America that we need to think about. It is between the Cares and the Care-Nots.

Cares worry about the spread of self-interested behavior and the misfortunes of others, and they want to do something about it. Cares exist on both the left and the right, and they have more in common than they realize. Cares on the left populate myriad antipoverty groups in the social justice sector—as do Cares on the right, who combat poverty at home and abroad through a vast net-work of faith-based charities. Conservative Cares docu-ment the toxicity of popular media—as do liberal Cares. At election time, Cares on the left urge Americans to get involved and heed higher ideals when casting their vote—as do Cares on the right. Liberal Cares write unending studies and books about the pressures on family life—as do conservative Cares, although they point to a different cast of culprits. Cares on the left talk about "downshifting" and dropping out of the consumer culture to live their val-ues—and you hear the same talk from evangelical Cares on the right.

The Care-Nots, in contrast, are insular and self-absorbed. Many have embraced the logic of self-interest as a way of life.

Research by the firm Environics and its founder, Michael Adams, suggests that the divide between the Cares and the Care-Nots has actually been growing more quickly than any other divide in America. Every four years since 1992, Environics has administered a household sur-vey in which more than 2,500 individuals spend three hours answering six hundred questions about their beliefs. According to Adams, the resulting data show that both conservative traditionalists and liberal idealists have been shrinking as a portion of the U.S. population. Which val-ues are growing? Adams argues there has been a growth in the ranks of Americans who reject nearly all authority and are focused on status, materialism, and risk-taking. They tend to be alienated, and turn to consumerism or violent media or high-risk sports to help fill the void. They are "resigned to living in a competitive jungle where ostentatious consumption and personal thrills rule." They don't vote. The Environics data show that this group has grown rapidly, nearly doubling during the 1990s from 16 percent of the U.S. population to 31 percent. Young people in particular are said to be moving in this direction.[4]

Adams's conclusions line up with what I found through my research for *The Cheating Culture*, which catalogs a rise in unethical, self-interested behavior across many spheres of American life. Other authors, including Jedediah Purdy in *For Common Things*, David Myers in *American Paradox*, Eric Uslander in *The Moral Foundations of Trust*, and Jean Twenge in *Generation Me*, have drawn similar conclusions. Some of Robert Putnam's research on community and social capital points in the same direction.

If it's true that more Americans don't care about others and are just out for themselves, this helps explain what is otherwise a great puzzle—pervasive moral anxiety at a time when so many social indicators have been moving in a positive direction.

RIGHT NOW, neither major political party grasps what is happening. Neither tries to speak to Cares on all sides of the partisan divide or offers a full account of why the Care-

Nots seem to be growing more numerous. Republicans offer a hopelessly narrow take on what has gone wrong while Democrats struggle to find a moral voice.

Democrats tend to make one of two blunders when dealing with values. The first is to accept the existing terms of the debate, stiffly quoting the Bible and scrambling to the center on issues like abortion and gay marriage. This may be a smart survival strategy in certain states or Congressional districts, but it doesn't get at the root of the problem or provide progressives with an authentic way to talk about values.

The second mistake is to plaster the values tag on the existing Democratic agenda, particularly in the economic area. Not long ago, for instance, I received a fundraising letter from Nancy Pelosi, the leader of the embattled Democrats in the House of Representatives. Declaring that Democrats were the defenders of "true American values," the letter called for more money for health care. More for child care. More for schools. More for unemployment insurance. Pelosi also pledged to protect pensions. Amen, I thought. There are certainly a lot of unmet material needs these days and, if you ask me, we must meet those needs to create a more moral society—an America where we look out for each other.

But what if you are also worried about other needs? What if you think of America as materially rich, but spiritually poor? What if you think that, yes, parents need more economic supports—and also protection from the bottom feeders who run our popular culture? What if you're all for affordable housing but don't think it will do anything to make neighbors more trustworthy? What if you agree that seniors should get the prescription drugs they need—and you worry about the overmedication of an entire generation of kids? What if—ever since the days of JFK—you've been waiting for a Democrat to ask you to do something for your country besides pay higher taxes? If this were the case, Pelosi's letter might leave you cold. Ditto for John Kerry's acceptance speech at the Democratic convention. Kerry used the word "values" eighteen times but never once did he hint at any defect in America's culture or suggest that anything other than more money was needed to strengthen family life or end poverty.

Even after their defeat in the 2004 election, the reflex of Democrats is toward the politics of bread and butter. That number once made them lucky, so they keep betting on it. If Americans can just see the clear economic facts, the logic seems to go, Republicans will be toast. Good luck, is all I can say. As 2005 came to a close, an ABC/ *Washington Post* poll found that nearly half of Americans thought the economy was in bad shape—but three-quarters were optimistic about their own family's financial situation. Earlier in the year, another poll found that 78 percent of respondents agreed that "Everyone has it in their own power to succeed."[5] Americans were optimistic even though most families haven't seen real income gains in four years, and even though the costs of housing, health care, and college tuition have been rising annually by double digits. Americans were optimistic even as many drowned in credit card debt, and even as two very dark clouds filled the horizon— the economic awakening of India and China, and the retirement of the boomers at a time when the federal government is already broke.

Why are Americans so optimistic? Because they are Americans. It's in their DNA. And because, for all their insecurities and debts, most have a phenomenally high standard of living. A while back I bought a decent sixteen-piece tableware set at Target for $9.99. "This is why the working class doesn't revolt," I told my wife, only partly in jest. Democratic messages about economic hardship have uncertain traction in a generally affluent society—except during those moments when the economy is really, really bad, like in 1992. At other times, Democrats are in the unenviable position of trying to convince voters that they are in worse shape than they think they are.

Economic appeals aren't useless by any means. Middle-class insecurity is growing and will keep growing as global competition intensifies, as technology replaces jobs, and as corporate policies siphon yet more wealth upward. People want help with health care, pensions, wages, college tuition, housing, and so on. But they want less tangible things, too. It's hard for Democrats to get a chance to address material anxieties if they don't address the nonmaterial ones. And, of course, even the economic concerns have a moral dimension. It's not enough to appeal to people's economic *interests*; you need to connect with their economic *values*. Democrats once were adept at challenging the self-interested excesses of the free market in ways that jived with American values around work and self-reliance. They haven't been so skilled at this lately.

THE GOOD NEWS for Democrats is that GOP dominance of the values debate can't last. Republican calls for moral renewal are appealing to moderate Americans in the abstract only. We like the idea of a moral bottom line, but we don't want that bottom line determined by Jerry Falwell. The actual details of the religious right's agenda, such as banning abortion and promoting abstinence-only sex education, do not enjoy majority support. To the extent that the evangelical base has enough clout to begin turning its agenda into policy—as it increasingly does—moderates will be scared off. We got a taste of this in the battle over Terry Schiavo. Even most Republican voters backed the decision to let Schiavo—who had been living in a persistent vegetative state for years—die and opposed intervention in the case by the federal government. A poll after the episode found acute public uneasiness about the right's moral values agenda, with a majority saying that Republicans were "trying to use the federal government to interfere with the private lives of most Americans." More generally, polls show that only a minority of Americans want government to play to a stronger role in enforcing certain values. Americans are "tolerant traditionalists," in author Alan Wolfe's words. We don't believe in heavy-handed attempts to tell people how to live their lives.[6]

The far-right libertarians in the GOP are also out of step with mainstream opinion. These folks may wield even more power in the party than the evangelicals, and they are bent on eroding the protections that shield ordinary Americans from the downsides of a market economy— whether it's the social safety net or labor rules or the regulations that safeguard food and drugs. They have gotten as far as they have, in part, because they connect with the public's belief in self-reliance. The rigors of a freer market have been seen as a welcome antidote to a "something for nothing" welfare state and the bad behaviors that go with idleness. In practice, though, most Americans don't actually want to get rid of the forty-hour workweek or turn Social Security over to Wall Street or starve Medicaid to feed millionaires. We believe in self-reliance up to a point. We also believe in taking care of one another.

As the Republicans veer farther from the center, Democrats—or perhaps a new third party—have a chance to forge a fresh moral vision that can redirect America's values debate and its politics.

This book offers such a vision. The chapters ahead look

at seven areas: family, sex, media, crime, work, poverty, and patriotism. In each area, I look at how the values of self-interest have grown too strong, fanning an ethos of "market individualism." I also propose how to push back against this trend and strike a workable balance between freedom and responsibility.

While Americans believe deeply in liberty, in both the economic and social spheres, we also believe in the common good. And right now, neither left nor right fully melds these two beliefs. Conservatives want few rules about how corporations must behave—even as they try to make all of us live by strict religious morality. Liberals resist limits on social freedoms—but happily heap regulatory burdens onto business owners who dream of independence. In an age of extreme self-interest, the left focuses on collective responsibility as our path to salvation, while the right dwells on personal responsibility. Most ordinary Americans know we need to have both to advance the common good. And the political party that recognizes this has the potential to dominate elections for decades to come.

I'm not ideologically neutral. I don't think the solution is for everyone to just get along. I've met a number of evangelical Christians in the course of writing this book, and I've nodded in agreement to some of what they have said while they've nodded in response to some of my views. I know that Cares on the left and the right share more common ground than they think. I also know that the conservative movement is taking America in the exact wrong direction. The more power the right gains, the more divisive America will become. Don't take my word for this. Just watch C-SPAN for a few hours. National politics is more viciously polarized than ever before. And, as political scientists Jacob Hacker and Paul Pierson have documented, it is hard-right conservatives who are mostly responsible for this shift.

Liberalism offers the best foundation upon which to build a moral center. It is liberals—working with moderates—who have historically fought to push back laissez-faire values and to promote the common good. In the past, liberals have naturally blended a commanding vision of freedom with strong expectations from all citizens. In doing so, they built bipartisan majorities for change.

Liberals have made serious mistakes in the past forty years. In a sentence, they have failed to think enough about either the downsides of social freedom or the upsides of economic freedom. But today, if anyone can check the rise of market individualism and spur Americans to look beyond self-interest, it will be a new breed of liberals—liberals who are second to none in their defense of the preeminent American value of liberty, and yet demand both personal and collective responsibility across every sphere of life.

Liberals shouldn't try to appease the reactionaries.

They should isolate them by reaching out to the vast ranks of moderate Cares who are now disenchanted with both parties. Listening to talk radio, you'd think we are a nation of ideologues. We aren't. Most Americans already support a blend of freedom and responsibility. One reason a lot of us have tuned out of politics is because neither political party stands for such a synthesis. The culture war turns people off as surely as the constant scandals and endless campaigns and negative ads. It is a war fought by absolutists. Some of these combatants don't believe every word they are saying, but fear that any concessions will be seized on by the enemy. A *New York Times* story reported that fierce ideological adversaries often get along well in the green room where they wait to go on Shout Television, and even end up as friends. Wouldn't you just love to know what Democratic strategist Donna Brazille and Republican senator Rick Santorum have to say to each other over a private breakfast? Sure you would. But as things stand, you never will.

I hope this book can help start a broader, more honest conversation about values. I advance strong views in the chapters to come, but I'm not an absolutist. I've tried to hear out those who see the world differently.

If we can get past all the shouting, building a moral center shouldn't be too hard. The public is already there. Now we just need to get our politics there, too.

CHAPTER TWO

Family Matters

To DRIVE SOUTH OF DENVER ON INTERSTATE 25 IS to see the new face of the American suburb. A decade or two ago, there was not much along this stretch of highway save for a vast prairie that ran up to the base of the Rocky Mountains. Now large swaths of the prairie are covered with new homes and shopping centers and gas stations. The growth is so fast here that the exits on I-25 aren't numbered sequentially but rather with gaps—exit 184 is followed by 187—in anticipation of new off-ramps yet to come.

Whole communities spring up in these parts in a matter of months. A quarter-million dollars will get you a good starter home in Castlewood Ranch, where the supermarket is still under construction but the elementary school is already finished. Twice that money buys a 3,500-square-foot palace in the golf village of Vista Ridge. The treeless and windswept cul-de-sacs don't look very homey, but developments like these are the emerging epicenters of family life in America. Places like Denver, Phoenix, Dallas, and Las Vegas have been called "American Dream cities" because their fast-expanding suburbs are drawing millions of young families in search of affordable homes, good schools, and open space. Colorado has been especially popular. Colorado Springs, a sunny city seventy miles south of Denver near the base of Pike's Peak, has more than doubled its population in the past decade.

This area is not just a magnet for families; it is also a magnet for organizations that purport to speak on their behalf. Scores of Christian evangelical organizations are based in and around Colorado Springs. Ted Haggard's New Life Church is here, a megachurch with twelve thousand members. So is the National Association of Evangelicals, which represents thirty million members. The International Bible Society has its global headquarters in the city. Promise Keepers, in Denver, is not far away.

And then there is Focus on the Family.

Right before I-25 enters Colorado Springs, a roadside sign invites motorists to drop by Focus on the Family's visitor's center. The fact that Focus has a visitors' center is a tip-off about the size and reach of this organization. Thirty years ago, Focus consisted of James Dobson—a preacher's son with a doctorate in psychology—and a part-time secretary. Now it has a staff of 1,300 and a $135 million budget, all dedicated to advocating on behalf of "traditional family values." Focus also publishes numerous books and a half dozen magazines. Every day five million Americans hear a short radio commentary by Dobson, and every week his column appears in over five hundred newspapers coast-to-coast. Dobson is widely seen as the most influential evangelical in America.

The visitors' center has drawn a million people since it opened less than a decade ago. Here you can load up on Dobson's many books on parenting and marriage, with titles like *Bringing Up Boys* and *7 Solutions for Burned Out Parents.* These books have a warmth about them, a friendly and supportive tone that tells parents that Dobson is on their side. But they also have an edge. Dobson argues that children need more discipline and that adults must commit more fully to the hard work of family, faith, and marriage.

I've come to Focus to meet with Glenn Stanton, one of the group's leading thinkers and writers. I had imagined him as a well-scrubbed straight arrow, perhaps with a blue blazer and a red tie. But he's not like that at all. Stanton doesn't look much past forty, and with his goatee and wire-rim glasses, he'd fit in at any Greenwich Village café.

Stanton was raised in a Catholic family but was born-again in his teens. He married at twenty, and spent his twenties working in a warehouse and raising a family with his wife, Jackie. (They have five children.) Stanton went to college at twenty-eight and then got a master's degree in the humanities. He has been at Focus on the Family since the mid-1990s.

Stanton has been studying marriage and the family for years, ever since Dobson circulated an internal memo that called for deeper research on these matters so that Focus would have an empirical foundation for its claims about the benefits of a strong family life. Stanton's explorations have led him to believe in these benefits more strongly than ever. As he sees it, there is an overwhelming "wealth of data that marriage matters" in terms of making people happier, healthier, and wealthier. While these arguments have received wide attention in recent years, Stanton's *Why Marriage Matters* came out in 1997, putting him ahead of the curve. Another thread of his work has examined what goes into creating a fulfilling marriage. Stanton argues that we now have a huge amount of such information, most of which is ignored. "We have the knowledge and we don't apply it."

A reason for this, Stanton says, is that most people don't think enough about the stakes of family life or make an effort commiserate with those stakes. People spend more time managing their careers and 401(k)s than their family ties. "It's hard work," he says. "It requires discipline. We need to sacrifice for others."

As a political force, Focus works closely with some of the most right-wing politicians in America. Many of the positions espoused by Focus are standard conservative fare: bring back creationism and prayer to the schools, ban same-sex marriage, outlaw abortion, repeal no-fault divorce laws, prohibit stem-cell research, teach abstinence-only to teenagers, and so on. If you ask me, this agenda is reactionary and repressive. But one doesn't have to be a homophobe or a "father-knows-best" type to connect with a core theme of the group's work, which is that it is very hard to raise good kids in this culture and hard to sustain a marriage. Focus offers advice about how to build intimacy with your spouse or talk to your teenager or save a troubled marriage or nurture your child's imagination or keep the bad influences of Hollywood at bay. It publishes colorful magazines for kids and teens that aren't filled with celebrities and models. It reviews films, television shows, video games, and CDs to alert parents about violent and sexual content. Evangelical views are slipped into these materials, not hammered home. You needn't long for a return to the 1950s to find this stuff appealing.

After all, where are the other champions of family life? In 2001, Democratic strategists Stanley Greenberg and Robert Borosage warned that parents don't just worry about their finances and don't just want help in the form of child care or health insurance. They also worry about their "ability to transmit basic values to their own children, who are enticed by an increasingly scabrous teen culture. They are looking for leaders who will help restore and reinforce these proper lessons. . . . Their concerns about individual responsibility and basic morality are likely to find increasing political expression."[1] Others on the left have made similar points, including Cornel West and Sylvia Ann Hewlett in their 1998 book *The War on Parents*. Yet somehow the message never seems to stick. For liberals, the economic woes of families tend to trump other concerns, and the language of bread-and-butter rules.

So it is that groups like Focus on the Family have had the field of "family values" largely to themselves for thirty years. Their focus has been exclusively on cultural challenges, and many of their complaints link back to the social earthquake of the 1960s. The main problem facing families is said to be liberalism. The solution? A return to traditionalism. It's pretty simple stuff.

What's missing from public debate is a more holistic story about what has gone wrong with family life. As Borosage and Greenberg rightly noted, the problem is not the economy *or* values. It's both, and they are wrapped up in each other. More personal responsibility, to better honor the selfless ties of love and kin, is part of the answer. More collective responsibility, to support families economically, is another part. Is this too much for us to process? I would hope not.

LET'S START WITH a simple fact: Most people want to have a strong marriage and a happy family life.

This is amply documented in any number of opinion polls. For example, large surveys of high school students—a key group, since they aren't yet married—find these young people overwhelmingly in favor of marriage and family. Belief in marriage, far from eroding in recent years, has actually grown stronger among teenagers since the 1970s. Surveys also show something else that bucks the conventional wisdom: Younger generations of Americans are more likely to prioritize family over work than older people. Young men in particular don't want to be the disappearing dad or absentee husband. Many want to share in the child rearing, even if it means making less money and having less career success. The differences across generations are notable: One study found that 82 percent of men in their twenties agreed that an important part of any job was having a "schedule which allows me to spend time with my family," compared to 67 percent of men in their forties. And if there once was a time when extramarital sex was viewed casually, that time has passed. Strong majorities of both genders say that such sex is always wrong.[2]

The notion that America's culture has turned against marriage and family does not square with the near-universal aspiration to have a strong family life. On the other hand, something is obviously very wrong, given that so many marriages end in divorce. The state of the American family is a paradox. We value marriage and family in principle. But in practice, a great many of us don't stick with our commitments.

Why is that?

One answer might come from my friend "Sam." He is a corporate consultant in his midforties, living on Manhattan's Upper East Side. He was married once, but things didn't work out. It is not that he and his wife were at each other's throats; they simply realized that they were very different and the relationship wasn't making them as happy as they would have liked to be. It didn't seem worth the work, so they went their separate ways. That was over a decade ago, and Sam has yet to remarry. He has plenty of female companionship and all the freedom in the world.

Sam is in no hurry to get married again, and he has been in a number of brief relationships since his divorce, cycling through a few women a year. This isn't the life that many people would choose, but Sam seems as happy as anyone else I know. He says, "Unlike, say, my brother— who is constantly running to take kids to soccer practice or go to recitals or to the in-laws' for dinner—I have more-or-less complete autonomy over my life."

Or take my friend "Jill." A little past forty, she also has no responsibility for anyone else. She has never been married, although she's had a few serious relationships where it looked like marriage was in the cards. While none of them worked out, that hasn't stopped Jill from having a full life. She has friends, makes a decent living, and owns her apartment. Sex is easy to come by even if love isn't. Jill very much wants to get married and is hoping that Mr. Right will soon materialize. Could she imagine getting hitched to Mr. Okay? Not a chance. As Andrew Hacker has pointed out in his book *Mismatch*, women are less willing to put up with men who are sexist, difficult, or just mediocre. Why should they?

Sam and Jill are the types of people who might be called selfish or hedonistic by a certain kind of culture warrior. They sleep around, haven't formed family ties, and are accountable to no one. And, oh yes, they are liberals.

The spread of this kind of lifestyle is typically blamed on the 1960s—the era of "if it feels good, do it"—or on the "me decade" of the 1970s, with its therapeutic focus on personal needs. Or, even more perniciously, on what William Bennett has called "the withering, sustained attack on marriage and the nuclear family" that emerged during this era.[3]

The real story goes back several centuries. Demands for individual autonomy have been growing in Western societies for three hundred years—ever since the Enlightenment introduced the idea that every individual has unalienable rights. For a long time, however, the amount of personal freedom one could realistically hope for was limited. Hardship was the norm for ordinary people, so they were inclined to take orders from those who helped keep them or their offspring alive: the church, political bosses, village elders, the police, government. Deference to hierarchy and traditional authority was the price you paid for basic security and survival. Obligation to family was another price, since blood ties were a person's only real safety net in case of health or financial problems. Pooled family labor was also key to keeping a household going, especially on a farm, where half of all Americans still lived in 1900. In these earlier times, in short, there wasn't much leeway to "do your own thing." Instead, you followed the rules, stuck close to kin, and prayed to God that everything turned out okay.

Things began to change in the 1900s with rapid industrialization, and particularly after World War II. By the 1960s, few people in most Western countries had to worry about the basics of a secure life: food, shelter, medical care, income. And many enjoyed much more than the basics. Unparalleled prosperity is the forgotten headline of the 1960s, buried beneath all the chaos. Forget Betty Friedan and Abbie Hoffman for just a moment to consider these facts about the 1960s: the gross domestic product soared at the fastest rate since the Gilded Age, the Dow broke 1,000 in the hottest bull market since the 1920s, and unemployment dipped below 3 percent while wages hit a record high.

In 1976, Daniel Bell offered an autopsy of the Protestant ethic—and the Puritan morality that went with it—in *The Cultural Contradictions of Capitalism*. Economic modernization had washed away small-town American life, Bell said, and along with it the "repressive threats of nineteenth century morality." Traditionalism was hard to sustain as America became more affluent and mobile, and more drenched in advertising, mass media, and consumerism. By the 1950s, Bell observed, America's "culture was no longer concerned with how to work and achieve, but how to spend and enjoy." This shift metastasized in the 1960s.[4]

Robert Bork tells a similar story in his culture-war manifesto, *Slouching Toward Gomorrah*, a book that otherwise blames liberalism for everything wrong in America. Once upon a time, Bork wrote, people were kept from "rootless hedonism" by the restrictions of "religion, morality, and law," as well as by the "necessity for hard work" and the "fear of want." But these "constraints were progressively undermined by rising affluence." This insight explains a lot, so it is rather mystifying that Bork mentions affluence only this once in his four-hundred-page tome about moral decline.[5]

The best evidence for the effects of affluence on people's values is found in the World Values Survey. Started in the early 1970s by political scientist Ronald Inglehart, the survey has periodically asked a growing number of people worldwide about their beliefs. (More than eighty countries have been surveyed.) Over three decades, Inglehart has documented how societies invariably move away from "survival values" and toward "self-expression values" as they become wealthier. In an age of affluence, Inglehart writes, "the disciplined, self-denying, and achievement-oriented norms of industrial society are giving way to increasingly broad latitude for individual choice of lifestyle and individual self-expression."[6] More wealth and security has also made people less willing to defer to authority, whether in the form of church or government. As Inglehart put it after reviewing data from dozens of nations: "We find a pervasive trend toward weakening hierarchical controls over the individual."[7]

All of these trends have dealt the family a major blow. A strong family is no longer necessary to keep income flowing, since families don't live on farms anymore. Nor must one have plenty of children so that a few will survive and provide care in one's old age. All you need now for decent golden years is a pension, Medicare, and a condo in Florida. (Bridge partners help, too.)

In a related trend, men have become less necessary. Women don't need men to ensure their survival, since they can now work outside the home in an economy where the good jobs require brains, not brawn. They can even get pregnant without a man—using the purchased sperm of a

Mensa member, no less. Men have exacerbated their dis-posability by lagging well behind women in attitudes about gender equality. Many men still insist on having the upper hand, whatever they tell pollsters. It was one thing to ask women to put up with this when they had no other choices; it's quite another when women are getting college degrees at a higher rate than men and when single women are twice as likely to purchase their own homes.[8]

In short, most people no longer face any economic im-perative to follow traditional norms. Yes, cultural views shifted to legitimize new social freedoms around family and marriage, but it is economic changes that have made these freedoms widely attainable. So perhaps "hedonistic" is not the best word to describe my friends Sam and Jill; maybe "rational" is a better word. They live as they do be-cause they *can*. If you want to see this phenomenon play-ing out in fast-forward, take a look at China these days, where modernization is charging ahead as in no other place in the world. The divorce rate in China climbed by 21 percent in 2004 alone. India's divorce rate is also soaring along with its GDP.[9]

None of this is to say that marriage doesn't matter. It does. Much research shows that the kids of intact mar-riages do better in life, and that married people are happier, healthier, and richer. Married people also report having more sex and better sex. These are good reasons to get married and stay married, but they are not nearly as pressing as the reasons people once had. If we don't *have* to do something, many of us just won't do it—whatever the lost benefits may be to ourselves, our children, and society. Thus the paradox that Americans believe in marriage and family as intensely as ever, but we often don't practice what we preach.[10]

Conservatives say they love capitalism because it promotes human liberty. Fair enough—as long as they acknowledge that when it comes to family, capitalism has yielded a lot more freedom than anyone bargained for.

Something else needs to be acknowledged, too. Market forces haven't only weakened the practical bonds that once tied us to family; these forces also corrode the very notion of obligation to others. In a society where everything is for sale, so to speak, we are told that we are fools to pursue anything besides our own agenda. Laissez-faire thinking holds that the best America—one with maximum wealth and human excellence—will emerge when Americans are encouraged to follow their own self-interest, guided only by the "invisible hand." Mutual obligation has been smeared as a naïve pipe dream, or worse, and we can barely turn on a television talk show without hearing that those programs that tie us to others—Social Security, say—run counter to common sense. For all the lip service to "personal responsibility," the message from many quarters has been that we should have responsibility only to ourselves.

These currents spell big trouble for family life, given that the obligations of marriage and children have become largely voluntary. The family values of "we" are a tough sell in an economy that is all about "me." As Nancy Folbre has observed in *The Invisible Heart*, strong family bonds depend on unselfish behavior motivated by love—altruism that often makes zero economic sense.[11]

In many ways, divorce is a perfect expression of market individualism and the consumer ethos. Why stick with a product if it doesn't work all the time, or if you have to break a sweat to make it work? Why hold on to last decade's model if there is a newer, better, or younger version now available? Why keep a product if it's a burden and if you imagine that you would be happier without it? Indeed, why even buy a product in the first place if you're not sure that you can't do better in a marketplace of many choices? Why not just keep shopping around until you're fifty, and then get a product half your age?

The great promise of consumer culture—promoted around the clock by $150 billion a year in advertising—is that we need never be discomforted or inconvenienced; that we need never put any whim or burning desire on the back burner, or accept anything less than an optimal experience; that we always have more choices, new choices, better choices.

Whatever else you may say about consumerism, whether you're pro-mall or anti-mall, one thing is certain:

This outlook is fundamentally at odds with the vows of marriage and the realities of parenthood. In even the best family life we are often discomforted and inconvenienced, and we are stuck with what we have—the jock we married when we were twenty-four and just a kid, the children who share our blood but not our temperament, the in-laws whom we might happily send on a cruise around the world. Family may be about any number of things; unlimited choice is not one of them.

Today about one-fifth of all marriages are over within the first five years—less time than many people hold on to a Honda. Some "starter marriages" end even more quickly, with one spouse bolting for the door within the first two years. And we all know of marriages that haven't made it past the first anniversary. Divorcing couples give any number of reasons for calling it quits, including such deal-breakers as infidelity or abuse. The most commonly cited reasons, however, have nothing to do with sexual hedonism or empowered women dumping abusive men. The leading killers of marriage are more prosaic: incompatibility, poor communication, money problems, and a plain lack of happiness. In earlier times such problems were endured, sometimes with positive results. As author Judith Viorst once commented: "One advantage of marriage, it seems to me, is that when you fall out of love with each other, it keeps you together until maybe you fall in again." Not anymore. Now many people bail as soon as the daily irritations of coexisting with another human being kick in, and so their love never gets a second chance.[12]

The effects of divorce is a charged and complex subject. Bringing up this topic can be a good way to ruin a perfectly nice dinner party. However, I think most of us can agree that it would be better if more couples got along, more marriages endured, and more children grew up in happy two-parent families. So maybe the right question is not "what is the fallout from divorce," but rather, why do some marriages work while others fail? And if there is a secret weapon that can defend the bonds of selfless love against the logic of self-interest, what is it?

ONE GOOD PLACE to start answering these questions is just down the road from Focus on the Family, in Colorado Springs. This city is among the most conservative and Christian places in Colorado. It was also recently dubbed "Splitsville" by a local paper, which noted that the divorce rate in El Paso County—home to the city and its suburbs—was 31 percent higher than the state average. The city is so well-known for its many divorce lawyers and divorced people that in 2004 *Men's Health* magazine gave Colorado Springs a "D" for its marital environment.[13] By contrast, the most liberal city in Colorado—Boulder— has a divorce rate well below the state average.

Why so many divorces in Colorado Springs? Nobody has crunched the numbers to fully answer that question, but there is enough broader research on divorce to suggest that religion is not the decisive factor in whether a couple stays married. In 2002, the Centers for Disease Control released an exhaustive statistical analysis of marriage and divorce. It found, as you might expect, that religious faith provides some buffer against divorce. The divorce rate for fundamentalist Christians clocked in at 44 percent, compared to 56 percent for those with no religious affiliation.

However, what correlated most closely with staying married, the study found, was income. Rates of divorce for women with family incomes under $25,000 were a staggering 65 percent—compared to just 31 percent for women in families making more than $50,000. Education levels were not far behind as a key factor. Sure enough, if you look at the difference between Boulder and Colorado Springs, you'll find that median household income in Boulder is much higher than in Colorado Springs and that over half of Boulder County residents have a bachelor's degree, as opposed to 31 percent of those in El Paso County.[14]

Scholars have long observed a link between marital stability and socioeconomic status, arguing that marital success has less to do with moral beliefs than with class position. Some researchers suggest that as economic stratification has grown, so too has a "divorce divide." In a recent study, sociologist Steven Martin analyzed divorce data from the 1970s through the 1990s, controlling for variables such as at what age people married. His findings were startling: The rate of marital breakup had plunged by almost half among people with four-year college degrees—and especially among women who'd been to college—while there was no decline among less educated people.[15]

In Colorado, where socioeconomic well-being has climbed rapidly in recent decades, the overall divorce rate has fallen substantially. The state's divorce rate dropped by a third during the 1980s and '90s, a period that correlated with an influx of young college grads who came to work in tech companies.

Data on who stays married fly in the face of conventional wisdom, at least as it has been purveyed by conservative culture warriors. The villains in their story have been educated feminists and hedonistic rich liberals. Listening to such rants, you'd think that married couples would be confined to zoos or museums in places like Cambridge or Berkeley, while lifelong monogamy thrived among the salt-of-the-earth types out in the heartland.

Now we know this is exactly backwards. Certainly the case against feminism doesn't hold up: The more educated a woman is, the less likely she is to get divorced. Also, if you look at trends in societal attitudes toward gender equality, they don't track with divorce rates. Divorce spiked to record levels in the 1970s, a period also famous for spreading feminism. Yet survey data from the National Election Studies finds that there actually wasn't much change during the 1970s in the percent of Americans who strongly believed in an "equal role for women." The big shift in views has come during the past twenty years, a period during which the percent of people favoring gender equality has nearly doubled. During this same time the overall divorce rate has declined.[16]

Some of the most liberal states in America have the lowest divorce rates. Nowhere is divorce rarer than in the District of Columbia, followed closely by the People's Republic of Massachusetts, the state that lately has been on the forefront of the same-sex marriage movement. Lifelong monogamy also thrives in New York and Connecticut.

On the other hand, look at Utah. The most Christian state in America and the one that gave Bush his biggest margin of victory, Utah has a divorce rate a third higher than that of Massachusetts. Wyoming, which Bush won by 40 points, has a divorce rate twice as high. As for the Bible Belt states, here we find some of the highest divorce rates in the union, mostly linked to poverty and the young age at which people get married in this deeply traditionalist part of the country.[17]

The marriage crisis in the red states may explain why moral values are so important to these voters. Family breakdown is a much bigger deal in their communities, and so they may be attracted to politicians who promise to make people behave. One thing is certain, though: The states with better-educated, wealthier people tend to have the lowest divorce rates, while the poorest states tend to have the highest.

Researchers haven't pinpointed the reason for this link (putting aside the age at which people marry), or why the link has grown in recent years. It might be that well-off couples are better communicators and more adept at solving marital problems with self-help books and therapy. It also seems obvious that more financial security translates into less stress on marriage and child rearing. Money is a notorious flashpoint for marital strife, and financial problems are a commonly cited reason for divorce. According to one survey of 21,000 married couples, "even happy couples disagree more about finances than any other topic." Some of these struggles revolve around debt, which has become a big issue. Americans carry record levels of personal debt, which traces to the growing gap between wages and the cost of living. Both partners in most new marriages now bring at least some debt to the altar—what has been called an "anti-dowry."[18] Money problems are often bound up in friction over how to balance work and family. If money is tight, the easiest way to earn more is to work more, which creates stresses on a relationship.[19]

In exploring why divorce tracks along class lines, one

researcher suggested that the problem is not that poorer couples are less happy in their marriages; they aren't. Rather, it's that these couples are more likely to get hit by financial setbacks and may be less able to handle the marital stresses that come with these crises.[20] When the going gets tough, rich couples can jet off to Paris and try to rekindle the spark. Poor couples will be lucky to afford two nights at Motel 6.

THE FINANCIAL PRESSURES on families are not exactly a state secret. And given how much attention they get, you'd think the folks at Focus on the Family would be working overtime on this problem. They're not. When I asked Glenn Stanton about this, he confessed that in all the years he has been at Focus there has been almost no conversation about economics and family life, other than work on financial education. "We tend to focus more on moral and cultural issues, and I don't know why that it is," Stanton said.

I pushed Stanton on this point. One of the biggest changes for families over the past four decades, I pointed out, is that a single paycheck is no longer enough to provide for a household and now both parents need to work. How could this shift not be part of his thinking?

"Do both parents really need to be in the workforce?" Stanton replied. He cited different ways that parents tried to pursue careers from home so they could put more attention on family. "Work is becoming the center of people's lives," Stanton said. People could change that.

Stanton also mentioned the problems with consumerism. He wasn't the only Christian conservative I talked to who advocated some form of "downshifting" to escape the materialism and careerism of American society and put family first. One doesn't tend to think of the Christian right as a countercultural force that is challenging consumer capitalism, but in some ways it is doing exactly that. This would seem a basis for common ground.

But even if the potential is there, it is hard to close the loop, as I found with Stanton. Those consumerist pressures are a natural part of capitalism, I suggested to him, and they are getting harder to escape. Also, since the free-market system has no inherent moral compass, didn't it make sense that it might operate in ways that undermine the family? And wasn't there abundant evidence of this everywhere— not just in the mismatch between wages and the cost of raising children, but also in the crazy schedules demanded by a 24/7 economy, or the insane commute times from the distant suburbs where many families lived, or the media culture pumped out to further corporate bottom lines?

Stanton seemed to agree with much of this, even as he dubbed himself a "thorough-going capitalist." But he didn't want to dig deeper with me, at least not as a spokesperson for Focus on the Family. "I wish we could engage this conversation about the dangers of capitalism,"

Stanton said. But it just wasn't part of his work at Focus—
or anyone else's.

IN THE SWEEP of history, married couples in America are
far better off than they were a century or even a half century ago. Life is better for nearly all families thanks to
modern medicine, indoor plumbing, electricity, larger
homes, and so on. As Stephanie Coontz has pointed out
in *The Way We Never Were*, spouses used to die on each
other all the time from diseases like polio and tuberculosis.
(Early deaths broke up more marriages in the nineteenth
century than divorce does now.) Also, poverty rates were
much higher fifty years ago, and per capita income was
much lower. Given all this, it seems silly to say that economic hardship is behind the high divorce rate. Yet if the
pressure cooker is less hot in absolute terms, the squeeze
on many couples is still intense—and seems to be growing
in some ways. Stressed-out parents have become such a
staple of research studies and bestselling books that sometimes it seems as though married America is having a collective nervous breakdown. Times may have been rockier
in the past, but they are plenty rocky today. What's different now is that there is far more focus on self-gratification
and far less need to be in a family. So it is more tempting
than ever to call it quits as soon as life pressures kick in and
a marriage turns difficult.

No one knows how to roll back individualism, which

has been gaining steam for three centuries, and no one wants to go back to a time when strong blood ties made the difference between life and death. On the other hand, we do know this: Better-off, more educated people are more likely to stay married. We also know that the divorce rate for this group has been declining. This points to at least one sure way to bolster family life: use public policy to reduce financial stresses on married couples.

Sounds like common sense, doesn't it?

If only. Families have gotten little help in coping with mounting economic pressures. You can see this right outside the front door of Focus on the Family. A recent study by a Colorado state agency estimated that the hourly wage a person needs to afford a two-bedroom apartment in Colorado Springs is $14.12. Many jobs pay much less than this. The study estimated how many combined hours a week a couple in that city would have to work at minimum wage to afford the apartment: 110. In Denver and Boulder it was closer to 150 hours. As in so many other parts of the country, family incomes have not risen as fast as housing prices in the state. "The bottom line is that many Coloradans cannot afford a home," the study concluded.[21]

Things are even more Darwinian when it comes to health insurance. If you don't have coverage through your job, you're in big trouble. The average cost of a family premium in Colorado is more than $10,000—too much money for many working families. Medicaid, the health insurance program for poor Americans, can't fill the gap. This program was never designed to help those with jobs and, in any case, Republicans in the state legislature have starved Medicaid to the point that Colorado ranks second to last in the breadth of its coverage. Without any health coverage, many families rely on emergency rooms and free clinics, but these services are in scarce supply, too.

The legislature doesn't just underfund Medicaid, it also has never fully funded the Children's Health Insurance Program, which is designed to cover children of working families. And, just for good measure, it has sometimes refused to fund the state Earned Income Tax Credit, which works in tandem with the federal EITC to ensure that parents who work do well enough to meet the basic needs of their family. (President Reagan once called the EITC "the best anti-poverty, the best pro-family, the best job creation measure to come out of Congress.")

To a visitor from outer space—or Western Europe— the shabby treatment of families by America's "pro-family" politicians might seem impossible to fathom. How can it be that these leaders talk endlessly of family values, only to leave families at the mercy of soulless economic forces that fracture marriages and hurt children?

This paradox is less inscrutable to anyone who knows America. We don't like to mess with the free market here, even to help families. And we tend to deny how much economic change has altered family life. This is why most par-

ents are now in the workforce—mostly out of necessity—
and yet the United States still lacks affordable child care or
paid parental leave. This is why we can slowly wave good-
bye to employer-provided health insurance and the average
cost of a family premium can soar into five figures, yet few
families get help on this front.

The American love affair with capitalism, whatever the
human toll, is well known. Less understood is the exact con-
stellation of values that makes Americans so brilliant at gen-
erating wealth and innovation—and so inept at protecting
families from the downside of economic competition.

I GOT SOME INSIGHT to this paradox when I headed south
from Colorado to the far more conservative state of Texas.
In Dallas, I had a long talk with Ann Hettinger, who is
the North Texas director of Concerned Women for America. Founded in 1978, CWA got going when Beverly
LeHaye, a born-again Christian, saw an interview with
Betty Friedan on television. LeHaye fumed as she watched
Friedan talk up the Equal Rights Amendment, and she
decided that feminists shouldn't be allowed to speak on behalf of American women. LeHaye set out to fight the "anti-
God and anti-family" forces gaining strength in America,
and to bring biblical principles into public policy. CWA
started "prayer/action" chapters around the country and
within three years had 100,000 members. Its first mission
was to defeat the ERA. It also led fights against abortion,

pornography, sex education, and the "homosexual move-ment." At one point, CWA members deluged the presidents of the three major television networks with two million postcards opposing condom advertising on TV.

By 1987 CWA had enough juice that President Reagan spoke at its annual convention. Today, CWA is a grass-roots powerhouse that's more than twice the size of the National Organization of Women, with an eleven-million-dollar annual budget, five hundred prayer/action chapters nationwide, and 500,000 members. It rightly calls itself "the nation's largest public policy women's organization."

Hettinger is a charming woman in her late sixties who grew up in rural Texas. She is a lapsed Democrat and a born-again Southern Baptist. Her husband is a partner in a major Dallas law firm, and when Hettinger is not doing her unpaid CWA work, she spends much of her time caring for her grandchildren. Family and faith are everything to Hettinger, and she sees herself as defending the family as God ordained it—the traditional nuclear family of a father, a mother, and children.

Hettinger readily acknowledges that economic changes have dealt the family a major blow. She traces the rising divorce rate back to World War II and later to women's entry into the workforce. "Then you had the two-income family, where mother has to work here and father has to work there, and they don't have any time for their children. Their ways parted, just like that. . . . In my day, in the area where I grew up, it took mother and father and all the children to make a home." Hettinger worked long hours alongside both her parents to bring chickens to market and can vegetables for the winter. "We were a family that worked together. We were a manufacturing unit. We took care of one another."

Hettinger longs for the day when women will give up the career track and recommit themselves to their "God-given role of taking care of the family." But she admits this isn't financially possible for most couples and doesn't think that will change anytime soon. "The economy is not going to turn around so that more mothers can stay home with their children," she admits. Through her own grown daughters, Hettinger knows well the struggles facing families. Does that mean she supports more active government help for families, like child-care subsidies? No. "Children are not wards of the state," Hettinger says. "Children are wards of their mother and their father."

As an example of how working parents might cope with the challenge of keeping their kids out of child care, Hettinger cites a couple she knows where the woman works nights and the man works days. "Their children are never in day care, because one of them is with them all the time." (Where sleep fits into this picture wasn't clear.)

Hettinger's views track closely with those of millions of Americans and underscore the enduring strength of traditional values in the United States. If you watch television or go to the movies or live on either coast, it is easy to imagine that traditionalism is not so strong in America. Conservatives themselves often paint a picture of a godless nation hooked on drugs and pornography. The reality is different. "America is one of the most traditional societies in the world," writes sociologist Wayne Baker, drawing on data from the World Values Survey. "Moreover, America's traditional values have remained relatively unchanged over two decades."[22]

These values have persisted even as Americans have often practiced something else and even as they have grown more accepting of different lifestyles. For example, nearly three-quarters of respondents in one poll agreed that "we should be more tolerant of people who choose to live according to their own moral standards even if we think they are wrong." Americans don't like to judge others.[23]

The United States is unusual in its traditionalism. Typically when countries get rich they dump traditionalism overboard for a "secular-rational" mind-set, an outlook that fosters pragmatic policy approaches to family and sex. The World Values Survey shows this trend in one country after another. Not here. Americans have all the social disruption that comes with advanced capitalism, and then some, but little of the rationalism. Mom now has to work—and often wants to work—but we long for the good old days when she could stay home with the kids. We long so much for those days that we won't adapt to reality.

America is the most individualistic, hedonistic, workaholic society on earth. But, because of the sway of traditionalists, we can't think straight about managing these conditions when it comes to our most important social institution, the family.

There is no easy way out of this jam. But if liberals and moderates want to change the meaning of "family values," they'll need a compelling definition of their own. They must combine two themes that now rarely go together: pushing people to take more personal responsibility and honor family ties, while also fighting to protect families in an ever harsher economic climate.

Many liberals are uneasy with talk of personal responsibility when it comes to family—not because they are against such responsibility, but because they see it as a guise for turning back the clock. They also worry that once you start putting any conditions on hard-won rights, you may set foot on a slippery slope toward losing those rights. This needn't be the case. While the concept of personal responsibility is often used to advance a repressive traditionalism, it can also be used to promote the humanist ideal at the heart of liberalism, which is greater obligation to others—even when this goes against one's immediate self-interest. Family life is one of the few spheres where market values have not entirely triumphed. Liberals should defend family, even as they redefine it.

One way to promote personal responsibility is through marriage education, a strategy that both liberals and conservatives can embrace. People need to hear—again and again, from a variety of leaders—that real work and sacrifice is required for happiness in love. They also need practical tools. Glenn Stanton's desire to spread the knowledge about "what works" to make marriages stronger could be echoed by any shrink in Greenwich Village. Hundreds of programs to aid couples are now offered across the United States. They are secular and religious, public and private, and use many different approaches. Some are better than others, and research analyzing their effectiveness stretches back at least two decades. Much of it is very encouraging. Still, these efforts only scratch the surface. Most couples don't have the orientation to do serious, informed work on their relationship or to get help when things turn sour. Some lack the money for counseling. A far larger investment by government and civil society groups in preparing people for marriage and strengthening marriage could yield major dividends. Advocates of scaled-up marriage education efforts have put forth an extensive agenda in this area. They outline ideas for increased funding of existing federal programs, new initiatives in schools and universities, public education efforts, additional research on what works, community organizing strategies, and much more.[24] Democrats should get behind this agenda in a big way.

Promoting responsible fatherhood is another key strategy. Traditional values have often served as a defense for the prerogative of fathers to dominate family life, but traditionalism also offers a way to control male selfishness—domesticating men, as it were—by binding men into the obligations of family. Amid all the new social freedom, we don't know how to do this anymore. Violent, antisocial, and self-destructive male behavior is everywhere. An economy in which men feel "stiffed," as Susan Faludi has written, worsens the problem, as does an onslaught of media images that equate money with status, leaving many men feeling disempowered. And then there is the pervasive consumerist ethos that stresses personal gratification above all else. No wonder so many men bail on family obligations the moment things get difficult. The cycle is self-fulfilling in that boys raised without fathers are more likely themselves to put self-interest first.

The Christian right has a plan to deal with wayward men and disappearing fathers: faith, discipline, and family obligation. Does anyone else? Yes, in fact. A range of efforts are now underway to promote responsible fatherhood. Some are connected to the African-American faith community. Others are secular and nonprofit. There are concerns that some attempts to renew fatherhood also seek to renew patriarchy, but that needn't be the case. The best initiatives to promote responsible fatherhood teach men to succeed in relationships of equality and respect. They also teach concrete fathering skills, help better connect incarcerated or divorced men to their children, and push for "father friendly" workplaces. In addition, these efforts help men build personal efficacy through educational and economic supports. Simply put, it's hard to be a good dad without a good job.

The notion that marriage and family can make men more responsible offers a powerful way to argue on behalf of same-sex marriage. Marriage, with all its legal and financial protections—to say nothing of its emotional benefits—is too important to deny to certain citizens based on their sexual orientation.

The freedom for all to marry is hard to win in the United States for a number of reasons. For one, we live in an age of rights fatigue. People are wary of the trend whereby freedoms keep expanding while obligations keep shrinking. Winning a new freedom as big as same-sex marriage may only be possible if it is linked to a strategy for promoting more responsibility. As author Jonathan Rauch and others have argued, the ability of gay men to legally marry could lead to more positive, committed, and healthy behavior. That is a very different kind of argument than an absolutist claim to more rights. So too is the argument that same-sex marriage will better enable homosexuals to honor their responsibilities to those they love, especially in moments of crisis.

A new conception of personal responsibility around marriage and family should be accompanied by an expanded vision of collective responsibility. Parents shouldn't be left to fend for themselves in a dog-eat-dog economy. Mothers shouldn't be marginalized in a modern workplace that is still at war with women who want both children and a career. Working parents need basic supports. They need paid family leave, not just to cope with a newborn or sick child but also ailing parents. They need affordable and high-quality child care, which can be very hard to find. They need universal health care so that they don't shortchange their children's health and don't risk personal bankruptcy if illness strikes. Also, we should return to a time when parents received more generous tax breaks.

These policies would shore up crumbling supports for the middle class and help America adapt—finally—to a postindustrial world where both parents often must work to make ends meet. Such ideas have been proposed for decades, of course, to no avail. That might change if liberals and moderates adopted a new language of responsibility—personal *and* collective—and emerged as powerful champions of marriage and family.

Those in the moral center won't convince the Ann Hettingers of America. But they can and should connect with the anxious moderates who heed people like Hettinger and groups like Focus on the Family because no one else is speaking to them.

CHAPTER THREE

Sex and Responsibility

AMERICA HAS LONG BEEN FAMOUS FOR ITS CURIOUS mix of Puritanism and libertinism. This is a nation where church members in a Missouri town recently protested a high school performance of *Grease*—too much kissing they said—while an episode of *CSI: Miami*, featured the murder of a teenage girl who had sex with two guys in one night. It is a place where one third of school districts now teach nothing beyond "abstinence-only" sex education—even as kids Google subjects like oral gonorrhea. It's a nation with some three million unplanned pregnancies a year—and yet it is easier in some cities to get Ecstasy than the "morning-after" pill.

These juxtapositions are growing. A full-scale revolt against sexual freedom is gaining energy in many parts of the country, driven by a deep religious conviction that any sex outside of marriage is wrong. Most Americans don't share this view. A strong majority embrace freedoms that were taboo a half century ago, such as cohabitation, and views on abortion haven't changed much in thirty years. Opinion on homosexuality has grown steadily more tolerant, polls have shown. At the same time, many people on both sides of the partisan divide are uneasy with the sexual climate, and for good reasons. You needn't be a prude to feel that things are careening out of control in this area, fed by an army of profit-hungry bottomfeeders.

Social conservatives stand virtually alone in voicing this anxiety. They appeal to the hard-core traditionalists who want to turn back the clock—and to plenty of ordinary Americans who are worried about so much sex and so little commitment, so much crudity and so little modesty. The new Puritanism is fed not only by a *Temptation Island* culture that turns tawdrier with each Nielsen sweepstakes; it has gained traction because it is filling a vacuum. There isn't much middle ground in the debate on sex. You seldom hear an affirmation of hard-won sexual freedoms that is coupled with equally clear calls for more sexual responsibility. "Yes, but," captures the view of most Americans, but the only choices seem to be "no," or "anything goes." Given that choice, many people will gravitate toward "no." And so the sexual counterrevolution keeps gaining steam: more federal funding for abstinence-only education. More state laws that chip away at abortion rights (some four hundred laws have passed since 1996). More pharmacists who refuse to carry emergency contraception. Is it hard to imagine new attempts to ban contraception or criminalize adultery? I think not.

Democrats, along with the dwindling ranks of "Planned Parenthood Republicans," have been caught in endless defensive battles. Whatever leverage they have in the sex wars comes mostly by tapping into fears of repression. We'll keep James Dobson out of your bedroom, and we won't let Sam Alito in, either. This approach goes a long way in a nation attached to privacy, but it's no answer over the long term. Liberals and moderates have their own qualms about sexual freedom gone awry—or should, anyway. And until they speak honestly, the reactionaries will rule.

Look, soulless pleasure-seeking was never the goal of the sexual revolution. The goal was to dismantle repressive attitudes that surrounded sex with fear. It was to de-link law from the strict religious beliefs of certain groups. It was to empower women to enjoy sex and have the control of their bodies necessary for full equality. It was to ensure basic liberties for all citizens, regardless of sexual orientation. These goals were about the common good, not unbounded self-interest. Even at the extreme edges of the 1960s counterculture, hedonism alone was often frowned upon, as Timothy Miller has shown in his book *The Hippies and American Values*. "Flamboyant self-expression was wonderful," Miller writes, "but one's first commitment had to be to the group, not the self." These days, as market forces work to strip the humanity from our ties with one another, the link between sexual freedom and lofty notions of the common good is fuzzy at best. Instead, sex is one more arena where an extreme focus on self-interest seems to have gained the upper hand.[1]

America needs to reaffirm sexual freedom and expand it in some places. We also need to clean up the mess that has come with this freedom. And while it's hard to imagine a cease-fire between NARAL Pro-Choice America and Concerned Women for America, I can imagine some unlikely allies banding together to battle the *Maxim* mindset and carry us away from the Paris Hilton era toward a new sexual humanism.

Before any of this can happen, however, we need to be more honest about our sexual history.

As with marriage, the historical memory about sex tends to go back only a few decades. Sexual freedom is often discussed as a recent cultural invention—another toxic by-product of the 1960s—that could be rolled back if we just pushed the right buttons. Of course, the roots of the sexual revolution run far deeper.

Even the Puritans knew that sexuality was hard to control in America. In his book *Sexual Revolution in Early America*, historian Richard Godbeer has shown that the Colonial era was rife with sexual struggle as moral authorities fought an uphill battle against extramarital sex, prostitution, polygamy, and illegitimacy. In the end, Puritan sexual morality was no match for the more individualistic approach to sex and personal fulfillment that became widespread by the end of eighteenth century. In the 1780s and 1790s, one-third of the brides in rural New England were pregnant at the time of marriage.[2]

The American focus on individual liberty fueled sexual permissiveness. So did a high level of mobility in a frontier nation of immigrants. If you're detached from your family and the community where you grew up, it's easier to be a little wild. For a long time sexual permissiveness was confined to men and channeled toward prostitutes. One hundred years ago, or even fifty years ago, plenty of young men made a point of losing their virginity as soon as they could, but they did so with prostitutes, not high school sweethearts. Nor is abortion a new phenomenon. It was common in the 1800s, along with out-of-wedlock births. The sexualization of children was also common in nineteenth-century America: The age of consent in many states was as low as ten, basically making pedophilia legal.[3]

None of this is to deny that the twentieth century ushered in major sexual changes: it did. But these changes started long before hippies and orgies, and—as with the related breakdown of marriage—economic and technological changes were key culprits in the decline of social controls. Automobiles, movie theaters, and amusement parks ushered in a modern era of dating where courtship occurred in public places, beyond family supervision. The title of Beth Bailey's book on twentieth-century courtship says it all: *From the Front Porch to the Back Seat.* The privacy offered by a parked car on a dark night was nothing short of revolutionary.[4]

Middletown, Robert S. Lynd and Helen Merrell Lynd's famous study of a typical heartland town of the 1920s, reported fast-liberalizing norms, and in 1926, F. Scott Fitzgerald commented that "the universal preoccupation with sex has become a nuisance." Freud's theories only worsened the nuisance. A survey taken in 1938 found that two thirds of women born after 1910 had lost their virginity before they were married. Abortion had become illegal by this point, but was commonplace and easily obtained if you were willing to risk death.[5]

The Great Depression put a damper on the wild times, but sexual freedom reappeared during World War II. The war turned American society upside down as 10 million men left their homes to fight and millions of women joined the labor force, disrupting traditional ties. The demands of a global war also elevated the role of science and rational analysis, furthering weakening the sway of faith and family. Premarital sex, adultery, divorce, and out-of-wedlock births were common in the 1940s. Alfred Kinsey's 1948 study found that nearly 70 percent of men had had premarital sex before the age of eighteen; a few years later he put the number for women at 50 percent. (Most of this sex was with future spouses, but not all.)[6]

The new permissiveness continued into the 1950s, as historian Alan Petigny has shown through a careful analysis of U.S. Census data. "Between the beginning of World War II and the inaugural issue of *Playboy* in 1953, the overall rate of single motherhood more than doubled," Petigny observed. "The silent generation may have been silent about what they were doing, but they weren't all that complacent." A great many unwanted pregnancies ended in abortion. Kinsey found during this period that a quarter of pregnancies among well-off white women ended in abortion.[7]

Given this history, it's silly to blame the countercultural radicals of the 1960s for inventing a new kind of irresponsible sexual freedom at odds with basic American values. As with the breakdown of marriage, the 1960s merely saw the (rapid) acceleration of a revolution that had been unfolding for decades. This remaking of sexual morality wasn't confined to America. It occurred across most of the developed countries as postwar affluence altered the values of younger generations, pushing aside traditionalism and survival values.

Other factors were at work, too. Advances in contraception technology finally broke the age-old link between sex and procreation. Forget John and Yoko lying naked in bed; their influence was negligible compared to that of John Rock and Gregory Pincus, the doctors who invented "The Pill," and G. D. Searle & Co., the drug firm that made a bundle from selling it. Or to the influence of the media barons, Hollywood moguls, and ad men who peddled sex for profit in one way or another. By the 1960s, even if you still lived in a small town in the Bible Belt it was nearly impossible to escape images of loose sexual norms.

Another culprit was an economy that compelled young people to get ever more education—a trend, in turn, that led them to marry later so that they could finish college, and maybe grad school. In 1950, fewer than 10 percent of high school graduates went to college and women married on average by age twenty. It wasn't unusual to tie the knot at eighteen. Today, nearly all middle-class kids go to college and women don't marry until their mid-twenties. The rare eighteen-year-old who talks seriously of marriage is packed off to therapy. Celibacy until marriage is a much higher bar to clear now that at least a decade yawns between the first race of hormones and any vow of lifelong monogamy.[8]

The cultural change of the 1960s and 1970s was far from irrelevant, of course. How else to account for the following statistic: In 1969, a Roper poll found that only 20 percent of Americans approved of premarital sex; just four years later, the public was evenly split on this issue. Yes, a revolution of consciousness did occur. But the fuse for this explosion was long burning.[9]

Another key fact to keep in mind is that while our mass culture does seem to get more salacious by the year, and expressions of teen sexuality seem to be changing, basic beliefs about sexual behavior very much stabilized by the early 1980s and haven't changed much since. While conservatives make political hay out of images of an unchecked slide toward Gomorrah, the facts suggest a different version of recent history. Data from the General Social Survey and the Gallup Poll show almost no change since 1982 in the percentage of Americans who take a permissive view of premarital sex, which stands today at about two-thirds of the public, just as it did when Ronald Reagan took office. "The Revolution is Over," proclaimed *Time* in a 1984 cover story about Americans and sex. "In the '80s, caution and commitment are the watchwords."[10]

There are plenty of good reasons to think that Americans do a terrible job of handling sexual freedom. What can't be denied is that this freedom reflects the national character. Or that it is embraced by most Americans. Or that it emerged in its present form as a result of major economic shifts that can't easily be reversed. The sexual counterrevolutionaries like to complain about liberal judges and Hollywood producers. If only things were so simple.

THE LEFT ALSO has to face up to some hard truths. The liberal reflex is to see sexual freedom as an unequivocal good. Because aspects of this freedom were so difficult to win, such as access to contraception, and because these freedoms never seem secure, liberals are loath to acknowledge any of its downsides for fear of ceding ground. This makes it hard to admit what is blindingly obvious: The ideals of liberation that were once associated with the sexual revolution were long ago pushed aside by an ethos that's about as enlightened as a strip mall.

Teen sexuality is exhibit A in what's wrong. The word from teenagers is that courtship and love are out. "Hooking up" in ways that avoid deeper intimacy, such as quick oral sex, is in. The dating talk of high school and college students is less filled with angst and longing; it is a more antiseptic conversation about "friends with benefits" and "keeping options open." Teenage romance once had little to do with control, at least as I recall it. It was about being human in the rawest way. Not anymore, according to many accounts. Maximizing choice seems to be the order of the day.[11]

Girls are often the losers in these deals. There once was a time when teenage girls explored their emerging womanhood only after poring over *Our Bodies, Ourselves* and deliberating with a consciousness-raising group about how to liberate themselves from the yoke of chastity. Now things are pretty ugly. Research and opinion surveys point to deeply damaging sexual dynamics among teens. The Alan Guttmacher Institute has found that one quarter of teen girls reported that their first experience of intercourse was unwanted and that the younger women are when they first have sex, the higher the chance that intercourse was unwanted or involuntary.[12]

Double standards of sexual freedom are alive and well. In a 2002 study, 87 percent of teenage girls said they experienced a lot of or some pressure from boys to have sex; 84 percent said girls often lost their boyfriends because they wouldn't have sex, while 92 percent said that girls got a bad reputation when they *did* have sex. The same study found that the burden of bringing up the topic of contraception or sexually transmitted diseases fell almost entirely on girls. While many adults are hesitant to say unequivocally that teenagers and sex are not a great mix, teenagers themselves believe exactly that. Over 90 percent agree that "most people have sex before they are really ready."[13]

Adults who came of age in the pre-AIDS era may look back nostalgically on their first taste of sexual freedom as a teenager. That was then. Sex is now a minefield for teens. Quite apart from the age-old fear of pregnancy, today's epidemic of STDs makes 1970s-era herpes fears look quaint. Kids are stalked not just by AIDS and herpes, but by a variety of other STDs that are flourishing at record levels, including chlamydia, gonorrhea, human papillomavirus (HPV), and syphilis. Three million teens get a sexually transmitted disease every year—that's *eight thousand new STD cases every day.*[14]

You might think that the answer to this sort of misery is better sex education for all teens and more empowerment of girls. And certainly that is an answer, as I'll discuss shortly. But beware the image of the healthy, sexually active teen. Research shows that the more psychologically well-adjusted teens are, the less likely they are to have sex. According to one study, teens with a very good relationship with their parents were 2.7 times less likely to have sex than those who didn't get along well with their parents. On the flip side, teenage girls with a history of sexual abuse were twice as likely as nonabused girls to have sex early, have multiple partners, and become pregnant. Also, the link between substance abuse and sexually risky behavior among teens is well documented.[15]

All this bad news aside, there is the bigger question of how healthy teenage sex can be in a culture where Paris Hilton can rise to fame on the strength of a homemade porn movie. Let's not fool ourselves about the kind of society we are living in right now. We live in the age of *The Bachelor*, not Aquarius. Sex is increasingly wrapped up in materialistic longing around money, cars, and clothes, or is simply the next jolt to clear an ever higher bar set by Xbox, text messaging, and other trappings of an overstimulated time. Boomer parents and teachers, with fond recollections of *Tales of the City*, simply have no idea what is going on.

Two thirds of TV programs contain sexual content, and that amount has grown in recent years. A 2005 study by the Kaiser Family Foundation found that the number of sexual scenes on television has nearly doubled since

1998. Those shows that are most popular with teenagers have the most sex in them. While Hollywood throws a bone now and then to the safe-sex crowd, messages about responsible sex are few and far between. Only one out of seven shows with sexual content include such messages. Research on the effects of media on sexuality is not extensive, but the studies that do exist lend credence to what seems intuitively obvious—that make-believe casual sex fosters real-life casual sex. Kids who watch a lot of sex on TV and the movies, some researchers suggest, are more likely to believe that sex without love is a positive thing, are more likely to be dissatisfied with being a virgin, and are more likely to have sex earlier than kids who aren't exposed to a lot of media sex. These findings are troubling not just because of all the unplanned teen pregnancies and the STD epidemic, but also because most kids who have had intercourse say they wished they had waited longer.[16]

Gender stereotyping is a related problem with the media. In one controlled study, exposure to even small amounts of Eminem's music was found to increase sexist attitudes in males. In many video games, the only women in sight are hookers or bimbos, and in *Grand Auto Theft III* the player can clobber a prostitute with a baseball bat. A content analysis of video games found that nearly a third of all women in such games were depicted as sex objects. Meanwhile, one of the big trends in magazine publishing has been the proliferation of quasi-porn magazines like

FHM and *Maxim* that objectify women—often quite literally, by surrounding scantily clad starlets with material objects that men aspire to own.[17]

If you don't believe the media influence our values, consider what recently happened in western Fiji. Within a few years of the arrival of television in the late 1990s, researchers documented a rise in eating disorders among teenage girls who had come to detest their bodies in comparison to the slim figures they were newly exposed to on the small screen. This experiment in how TV can reprogram personal values was hardly surprising. Here in the United States it has been estimated that 78 percent of all seventeen-year-old girls are unhappy with their bodies, and researchers have found that such unhappiness is correlated to media exposure. The more media kids watch—girls and boys alike—the worse they feel about their bodies. (The same goes for adults, by the way.) In one study, fifth graders reported more dissatisfaction with their bodies after watching just a single Britney Spears music video or a short clip from the sitcom *Friends*. Another study found that kids who identified with media celebrities—whether television stars or models or athletes—tended to be less satisfied with their bodies. All this may explain why teenagers had more than 300,000 cosmetic surgery procedures in 2003.[18]

Whatever sexual freedom may have meant in 1969 or 1979, it means something very different in an era in which

Ms. struggles to survive, while teens read *YM* and *Cosmo-GIRL!* Liberals must update their thinking. The enemy is no longer just a repressive traditionalism that peddles fear and shame; it is also a hypercapitalism that degrades and commodifies human sexuality. Sexual freedom is a dangerous thing in a climate where self-interest is king, where the mass media fan our basest instincts, and where just about every activity has been turned into a race for wealth or status.

Are liberals betraying their core ideals by pointing this out? Not at all. They are defending those ideals.

RELIGIOUS CONSERVATIVES win clout by demanding personal restraint in the face of a carnal free-for-all, and they have the audacity to imagine that they can actually change the culture. No one else suggests anything of the sort. Calls for modesty by the Christian right draw nods of approval, even among those who don't like the fine print about Antonin Scalia policing their private life.

The vacuum in the center helps to explain why bad public policy has scored so many triumphs in recent years. You can see this in the culture-war flashpoint of sex education, where abstinence-only education has been spreading rapidly even though most Americans say they back a more comprehensive approach. In 2001, a survey of school superintendents by the Alan Guttmacher Institute found that 35 percent of school districts require abstinence to be taught as "the only option for unmarried people, while either prohibiting discussion of contraception altogether or limiting discussion to contraception failure rates." Just 14 percent of school districts take the kind of comprehensive approach that research shows to be the best way to delay sex, stop the spread of STDs, and reduce pregnancy. Abstinence crusaders are rolling over Planned Parenthood types who have social science on their side but offer no moral bottom line.[19]

Something similar is happening in the abortion debate. However divided Americans may be on abortion, everyone can agree that there should be fewer abortions. We can all agree that it's a good thing that the U.S. abortion rate has fallen over the past twenty-five years and in 2000 reached its lowest level since 1974. What we can't agree on is how to push the rate lower, and many common-sense policies that could do exactly that never get brought to the table.

To listen to conservatives, you'd think that stronger religious beliefs and restrictive laws would stop abortions. But there is no evidence to support either proposition. Born-again Christians in the United States have 170,000 abortions every year, far more than the entire population of Canada has. Catholics account for 27 percent of all abortions. Looking abroad, some of the lowest abortion rates in the world are found in the largely secular nations of Western Europe, while some of the highest are found in the deeply Catholic nations of Latin America.[20]

Nor do laws have much impact on abortion. About 46 million abortions are performed worldwide every year, and nearly half occur in countries where abortion is illegal. Abortion is a pretty simple medical procedure—simple enough that it was commonplace a century ago, before the advent of modern medicine. Setting up shop as an abortionist requires neither specialized technology nor particularly advanced training. Brazil, Chile, and Peru all ban abortion, yet have abortion rates up to twice that of the United States. In contrast, a 2003 study found that some of the "world's lowest abortion rates are in western countries where abortion is not only legal but also covered as a standard service by national health insurance systems."[21]

Reducing the demand for abortion—i.e., reducing unwanted pregnancies—is both hard and easy in an advanced capitalist nation. Powerful market actors fan people's libidos 24/7, glorifying casual sex and objectifying both women and men as never before. Economic forces keep young people single longer and make marriage optional. If sexual responsibility is defined as no sex with anyone until marriage, good luck.

On the other hand, drastically cutting unplanned pregnancies, which now run at about three million a year in the

United States, is something we can do. We have the contraceptive technology, or can develop it. We have the marketing knowledge about how to encourage contraceptive use, including the "morning-after" pill. We have the national resources. If we want people to exercise more responsibility around sex and have fewer abortions—*many* fewer—we know how to achieve these goals without giving up a woman's freedom to control her body.

Western Europe makes this look easy. In Germany, France, and the Netherlands, the abortion rate is two or three times lower than in the United States. The gap for teenagers is even greater. German teenagers have eight times fewer abortions than American teens, while Dutch teens are seven times less likely to have an abortion—even though European teenagers are nearly as sexually active as American teens and it is easier to get an abortion in much of Europe than in the United States.[22]

How does Europe achieve some of the lowest abortion rates in the world? Rational public health policy, that's how. Unbiased research drives policy toward sexuality, with religion playing little role. Contraception—including emergency contraception—is available to all, especially teenagers, at no cost and with no hassles, through national health insurance systems. Comprehensive sex education begins in the early grades and is integrated into teaching on different subjects, as opposed to being shoved into a single forgettable class that is too little, too late. Sex is more likely to be the subject of open and honest conversations. Families tend to be closer, and may exert more influence on young people. Also, whereas the United States lets private industry largely control the sexual values messages coming from media, European governments use the media for big public education campaigns stressing sexual responsibility.

This is what "pro-life" policies look like in much of Western Europe, and they work. Core sexual freedoms are protected, but individuals are pushed to take personal responsibility—and given the tools to do so.

The United States isn't Europe. We have more poverty, among other things. Just because Europeans can balance freedom and responsibility when it comes to sex doesn't mean we can. But couldn't we at least try their approach?

I posed this question to Lorrie Parker, a leading pro-life organizer in Kentucky. Parker is a pale and soft-spoken woman in her early forties. She grew up in an evangelical home in rural Kentucky and is a devout Christian. Like many pro-life activists, her beliefs about abortion flow from her religious faith, and you can't spend ten minutes talking with her without believing that she is deeply committed to advancing God's vision of more compassionate world, as she interprets it. Respecting all human life is the key to such a world, Parker believes.

Parker started out as a volunteer in the pro-life movement and now receives a small salary for heading the Right-to-Life of Central Kentucky. She manages four or five volunteer workers in modest offices in a brick building in a suburban office district of Lexington. Kentucky's pro-life movement has never had more than a handful of paid activists across the state, but it has scored major gains in the past decade, including the passage of a parental consent law and a ban on late-term abortions (later voided by a federal court). If *Roe v. Wade* fell, the several abortion clinics in Kentucky—all in Louisville and Lexington— might quickly close.

Parker didn't know much about the public health policies of Western Europe, and she didn't dispute the basic facts about their success in lowering the abortion rates. Such details, though, didn't much matter to her. "That approach wouldn't work here because of our Christian beliefs," Parker told me. The United States simply could not sanction sex among unwed teenagers through public policies that provided contraception on demand, nor let the schools play such a large role in teaching young people about sex. "We have to follow biblical principles," Parker said, "since those principles are the basis of our nation."

I pushed her on this. Public opinion on abortion hadn't changed much in thirty years, I said. Large numbers of abortions continue year after year amid a political deadlock that is never broken. Even if *Roe* is overturned, the states where most abortions take place—such as New

York and California—would still allow them. So why not go with a strategy that is fairly certain to reduce the number of abortions?

Parker didn't take the bait. She said that we can't work at cross-purposes, implicitly promoting sex without commitment in order to get people to behave more responsibly and have fewer abortions. "That sends a mixed message."

Parker's views are not uncommon in the pro-life movement. These views have an internal logic. If you believe that sex outside of marriage is wrong—or even, as many conservative Catholics believe, that nonprocreative sex is wrong—then there is not much room for a "research-based" approach to sex and public policy. If teen sex is wrong, how can we teach anything but abstinence in our schools? If nonprocreative sex is wrong, how can we use public funds to pay for contraception? And if modesty dictates that sex stay private, how can we mount large public education campaigns on the topic?

This logic may be consistent, but ironically it works against the goal of reducing abortion. We can't turn back the clock, even if we wanted to. Traditional values aren't strong enough to stop tens of millions of Americans from having sex outside of marriage—even evangelicals and Catholics. These values aren't strong enough to reverse a three-hundred-year drive for more personal autonomy or to serve as much of a counterweight to market forces that fan a self-centered, consumerist sexuality.

Regardless of whether you think the sexual revolution is a good thing, it does show all signs of being permanent. We need to learn to contain its worst fallout. While people like Lorrie Parker are entitled to their beliefs, they should not be making public policy in the twenty-first century. However, until others come forward with a new moral language that addresses the intense public anxieties about sex, it is these activists who will drive the debate.

ABORTION IS BAD. Modesty is good. Teenagers should wait to have sex. Everyone must be responsible.

Most Americans don't want to repeal the reproductive rights and sexual liberties won since World War II, but they do embrace a set of judgments of this kind and want their leaders to state them out loud. Those in the moral center must articulate a forceful message about sexual freedom and the responsibilities that go with it. Such a message would not draw on the repressive (and failed) Puritan tradition, but on the liberal idea that every human being has inherent worth and dignity, and that no one should be merely the means to someone else's ends—whether it's for pleasure, power, or profit. Today's hypersexualized culture is clearly at odds with the values most liberals cherish. It tends toward misogyny and commercialization; it celebrates physical appearance over soul and character. It often doesn't bring people any closer, but instead leaves them feeling empty and depressed. In a true community we would connect to each other in more meaningful and respectful ways. So, yes, we do need to change this culture, and if reasonable voices said as much, the extremists on the far right would lose much of their clout.

Nothing good lies in the other direction. Unless a new center is defined, and quickly, America will continue its drift backward to an earlier time when religious dogma dictated public policy on sex.

Restructuring the abortion debate is a priority. Most Americans are moderates on abortion and this hasn't changed much in thirty years. In a debate between black and white positions, Americans prefer gray. They don't like abortion but support the right to abortion with various caveats, and they don't want to overturn *Roe*. Yet, when it comes time to vote, many grays gravitate toward the conservative pole—not because they have hard-line views of what the law should be, but because they share the conservatives' opinion that abortion is a bad thing.

In a new moral center, legal access to abortion should be defended as a social good. Society will be a better place if couples can decide when to have children or how many children they want. We all benefit when these decisions are made responsibly and when all children are wanted and loved. The ability to control fertility has been central to the betterment of humankind; abortion is essential to this ability. That said, abortion is clearly a bad thing because it is the worst possible way to manage fertility. It is often emotionally difficult for those who have the procedure and it is deeply troubling to many Americans—so much so that divisions on this issue are undermining the nation's political cohesion. For these reasons, a commitment to reproductive freedom should be linked inextricably with a responsibility—both personal and collective—to reduce abortions. If all sides explicitly embraced this goal, it might be possible to shift the debate away from the morality of abortions and to the practical question of how to prevent them in a manner most consistent with American values. Draconian steps that criminalize doctors and women and empower government authorities to control people's lives, would not be the first choice of a society where distrust of authority has historically run high and has risen in recent decades. Nor would this approach work best, given what we know from the experience of other countries.[23]

More effective, and more popular with Americans, would be an alternative approach that emphasized reducing abortion by stopping unwanted pregnancies. This would include comprehensive sex education, expanded health insurance coverage for contraception, new investments to create more effective contraceptive technology, public education campaigns to encourage responsible sexuality, increased government funding for family planning services, and ready access to emergency contraception without a prescription. Another way to reduce abortions would be to provide more support to women who give their children up for adoption or choose to keep them.

Finally, abstinence among teenagers should be promoted as a way to prevent abortion, as well as other negative outcomes, such as STDs. A large majority of kids say that teenagers are not ready for sex, and adults should listen to them more closely. Right now, most of the abstinence programs floating around have been developed by conservatives who oppose premarital sex for religious reasons. Many of these programs contain misleading information and rely heavily on fear. Kids need better guidance on why, and how, to have sex only when they are ready and can do so responsibly. It's not enough to criticize the bad abstinence efforts; we need to be more serious about developing and promoting efforts that work, and that go hand in hand with wider access to contraception.

Dozens of ideas sit on the shelf that could cut U.S. abortion rates overnight, as well as lead to a healthier sexuality among Americans. Liberals and moderates tout many of these ideas already. If they want more people to listen, they'll need to embrace a new moral bottom line about freedom and its responsibilities.

CHAPTER FOUR

Tipper Gore Was Right

W HEN MTV SET OUT TO CAST THE SECOND
year of its hit reality show about sweet-sixteen
parties, one of its producers, Megan Galloway,
put a posting on a Web site called Partypop.com. The site
is often used by rich teens planning birthday bashes, and
the message from MTV was aimed squarely at the wealthiest of them all. Galloway explained that the show, *My
Super Sweet Sixteen,* was documentary-style and follows
fifteen-year-olds as they plan their milestone bash. MTV
didn't help plan the parties or pay for them. If you wanted
your party featured in the series, you needed to be thinking big: "The party has to be a huge event (money is no object for your family)," Galloway said.

Galloway and her colleagues eventually settled on a
group of lucky kids, and the second season premiered in

August 2005. The episode attracted a startling 3.5 million viewers, and drew more young people than anything else on television during the half hour it aired.

I caught *My Super Sweet Sixteen* later in the fall, and it fascinated me in a macabre sort of way. It featured two different parties, one for a girl named Sophie and the other for Amanda.

Sophie's parents were loaded, and ready to spend any amount of money to placate their daughter. They bought her a new white Audi for her birthday, wrapped with a red bow—after Sophie made it clear that any sort of used car was out of the question. And they went all out for her sweet-sixteen party, so much so that the final bill was over $180,000. Throughout the party planning—getting the dress fitted, picking the live entertainment, deciding on the invitations—Sophie was often blasé and barely interested, as if this sort of event happened every day. Or she was petulant, cursing constantly. At one point her mom calmed her chubby daughter with a box of Dunkin' Donuts.

Amanda was just as foul-mouthed and nearly as unbearable. She said that one of the ways she got happy was by looking in the mirror. "I'm the kind of popular girl that all the other kids envy," she said proudly. Her father had made big money in business, and he carried around wads of cash that he lavished on his little girl. He sent her down to Miami with a few friends and thousands of dollars to buy a birthday dress. He flew in the R&B performer Ciara to perform at her party. He let Amanda invite nearly everyone in Ocala, Florida, where the family lived, to the event, which cost over $200,000. He also got on his daughter's nerves to the point that she told him, "Sometimes I want to punch you in the [bleep]ing face." The father just smiled and held up a handful of $100 bills, cooing her name. Amanda gazed at the money. "I can never stay mad at him for long," she said.

There was nothing ironic in the MTV show. No subtle mockery of the girls' unpardonable behavior, no sly outrage about the extravagance of blowing a fortune on a kid's birthday party. If there was a value judgment here, it was positive: Look at how cool these girls are. They are cool enough to know what a Versace dress is; cool enough to want an Audi, not a Saturn; cool enough to curse like a sailor, even at their own parents. The show was celebrating these girls, not knocking them, and several million kids across America were savoring every moment.

MTV doesn't feature much music anymore. It's jammed with offerings like *My Super Sweet Sixteen* or *Laguna Beach,* which also focuses on self-absorbed rich kids. Or it revels in backstabbing in *The Real World* or Darwinian competition in *The Gauntlet 2.* Or it's drooling over the luxury homes of celebrities in its show *Cribs.*

MTV is the number-one television choice among teenagers. And, if you ask me, much of its programming is pure poison. Millions of Americans—particularly parents—agree with that judgment, but the only groups who consistently slam MTV are on the right. These attacks, not just on MTV but on other programming, tend to dwell narrowly on sex or vulgarity, and their effect is to set off alarm bells among liberals worried about censorship. Battles over media and popular culture are as predictable as a game of tick-tack-toe. Social conservatives flip out about what can seem like minor indecencies, while liberals warn of impending theocracy. It's always the same rerun: the Bible versus the First Amendment, and usually the latter prevails. Nevertheless, it is conservatives who get the better of these tussles. When the right complains about the media's descent into tawdriness, it puts them on the side of most Americans.

Democratic politicians who take aim at trash culture are few and far between, and they tend to be centrists— senators Hillary Clinton and Joe Lieberman come to mind. The left wing of the party is mostly mum, or worse. When senator Al Gore's wife, Tipper, went after misogynist music lyrics in the mid-1980s, she was ridiculed for years afterward in liberal circles. In effect, conservatives have a near-monopoly on one of the most commonsense arguments you can make in American today: It's time to clean up mass media. This argument connects especially well with married people and parents—not a minor point given that the Republican edge with such folks is a key to their current dominance.

Despite high ratings for some of the most risqué and violent shows on television, poll after poll finds that a strong majority of Americans are deeply alarmed by trends in popular entertainment. A 2004 survey by the Kaiser Family Foundation found that 89 percent of parents were either very concerned or somewhat concerned that children are being exposed to too much inappropriate content in entertainment media. Eighty-three percent said that exposure to sexual content contributed "a lot" or "somewhat" to children becoming involved in sexual situations before they're ready, and 81 percent said that TV violence contributes to violent behavior in children. A large majority of parents in this poll said they favored new regulations to limit sex and violence on TV during the early evening.[1]

Parents aren't the only ones who want to do something about the trash culture. A 2005 poll by the Pew Research Center for the People and the Press found 69 percent of all Americans supporting bigger fines on broadcasters who show indecency and 75 percent favoring stricter rules on TV content when children were likely to be watching. While Republicans were more enthusiastic about such measures, strong majorities of Democrats also favored tougher steps. However, most of the survey respondents didn't believe that government restrictions would be effective, and nearly half said they worried more about government imposing undue restrictions than about harmful media contact. The vast majority of respondents thought a stronger parental role was the best way to defend children from inappropriate media content. Also, the poll found that 60 percent of people held a favorable view of the entertainment industry, and far more blamed audiences for trashy media products than producers—in other words, we get what we want. This last point might seem amply confirmed by Nielsen ratings. In May 2005, *Desperate Housewives* hit a high water mark when over 26 million viewers tuned into a Sunday-night episode—a quarter of all households watching television that evening.[2]

Obviously American views about the media are complex. There is a love-hate affair. People feel there is too much freedom here and not enough responsibility. Many also understand that self-interest and the bottom line is a big driver of cultural pollution. At the same time, they enjoy the fruits of this freedom and tend to think that the best solutions lie in changing personal behavior.

Conservatives don't trifle themselves with such nuances, and they aren't in the business of finding a sensible middle ground. Their specialty is straightforward moral outrage about offensive media. That stance is one more reason why polls give the GOP a double-digit edge over Democrats on such moral basics as knowing the difference between right and wrong and promoting personal responsibility.

Stanley Greenberg and Robert Borosage, in their 2001 blueprint for a liberal comeback, commented, "Progressives should be unabashed in criticizing a culture that peddles sex and violence, that substitutes sensation for reason and scandal for analysis."[3] Negative cultural influences, they noted, worried parents almost as much as all the economic pressures they were under. This advice, which seems pretty self-evident, didn't take. When it comes to Hollywood, many Democrats seem to think we're still living in 1962 and that cozying up to Tinseltown will help them gain favor with ordinary Americans.

Witness the way John Kerry shot himself in the foot at a star-studded fundraiser at Radio City Music Hall during the 2004 presidential campaign by telling a group of Hollywood entertainers that they "conveyed the heart and soul of the country." Kerry's words turned out to be a priceless gift to the Republicans, right up there with his windsurfing outing on Martha's Vineyard. A few days later, at a campaign stop in the Midwest, President Bush unveiled a new applause line. The heart and soul of America was *not* in Hollywood, Bush said. "I believe the heart and soul of America is found in places right here, in Marquette, Michigan." Over the next three months, the town or city that housed America's heart and soul changed constantly as Bush reminded audiences that John Kerry lived on Planet Liberal. "Most of us don't look to Hollywood as the source of values," Bush stressed in October. Along with Kerry's sail board, his $8,000 racing bike, his eccentric billionaire wife, and—well, the list was pretty long—his ties to Hollywood confirmed the most devastating claim of the Bush campaign: The senator from Massachusetts was one of Them, not one of Us.

Even after this debacle Democrats still didn't get it, as a top Kerry campaign organizer in Maine, Justin Leites, found out not long before election day. Leites was doing his best to keep this swing state and its working-class whites firmly in Kerry's column when he got a call from a top official at Kerry headquarters. She told him that the campaign was sending Sharon Stone to Maine to stump for Kerry.

Leites flipped out. He'd been coming to Maine all his life and knew how people there thought. Sending Stone around was a surefire way to turn them off. If Kerry wanted to help himself in the state, he should come up for a hunting trip. What he should *not* do is associate himself with the star of *Basic Instinct*.

The Kerry aide was insistent. She said that Paul Newman was campaigning door to door in Ohio and it seemed to be helping. Stone had name recognition. She also had a compelling personal story about rising from modest means. Sending her to Maine was part of a smart "surrogate strategy." The conversation turned into a screaming match before Leites was able to negotiate a compromise. Stone could stump in places like Portland, but had to stay far from the rural towns of northern Maine.

The pummeling liberals take as the defenders of cultural pollution is deeply ironic. After all, isn't it liberal researchers who first documented the negative impacts of violent TV programs and sexist advertisements? How did these arguments end up in Rick Santorum's mouth while Teddy Kennedy stayed silent? I've seen plenty of Volvos with "Shoot Your Television!" bumper stickers; I haven't seen many on Ford F-150s.

Also, isn't it liberals who have traditionally sounded the alarm about the corporate takeover of culture? To the extent that most of the bile bubbling out of Hollywood is designed with one goal in mind—to make money—it stands as yet another example of how unfettered self-interest can undermine the values we all care about. You'd think liberals would welcome a chance to point this out.

For instance, the money chase explains how Janet Jackson ended up exposing her breast for two seconds at the 2004 Super Bowl. The most profitable media programs, whether football games or sitcoms or radio talk shows, are those that attract the viewers advertisers most want to reach. Right now, no group of viewers is more prized than young adults ages eighteen to thirty-four, and it is common knowledge among media executives that risqué content is the best way to draw them in. So it made sense that Viacom would turn to MTV to produce its halftime show for the Super Bowl. And it made sense that MTV would go with a performance by two sexy stars that would have been plenty racy even without a "wardrobe malfunction." As author Robert McChesney has pointed out, Viacom is the "most commercialized of our media companies. . . . More than any other media company, its revenues depend upon ad sales from radio and television and cable. . . . And if you look at MTV in that context, you get a sense of what they're all about."[4]

A similar motive explains violent programming on any given day of the week, as economist James T. Hamilton explains in his book *Channeling Violence: The Economic Market for Violent Television Programming*. Young men especially love gore, and advertisers love young men. "Advertisers are willing to pay a premium for these viewers," Hamilton writes, "which means that some programmers will face incentives to offer violent shows."

Other research has shown how the trend toward more concentrated ownership of radio stations has led to an increase of risqué content on these airwaves. Corporate media groups are more focused on the bottom line and more willing to do whatever it takes to attract listeners. One study, which looked at the years 2000–2003, found that "eighty-two percent of the radio programs that generated FCC indecency fines were owned by a large, vertically integrated radio station ownership group." Clear Channel and Viacom were among the biggest offenders.[5]

And, of course, we all know about how the profit logic of "if it bleeds, it leads" drives news programming. Studies find that news shows portray crime as much more common than it is, creating exaggerated fears among the public. The nightly mayhem is good for ratings and terrible for social trust. Don't take my word that the bottom line has corroded news: Surveys show that most journalists believe the same thing. They see market values as pushing out the quest for truth or insight.[6]

Conservatives are reluctant to offer any critique of market forces, no matter how low they pull our culture. Liberals aren't, and it is liberals—along with moderate Republicans of earlier eras—who can take credit for creating public broadcasting as an alternative to commercial media and for passing federal regulations aimed at holding mass media accountable to the public interest.

Exactly how the Democratic Party came to align itself with an anything-goes entertainment industry run by bottom-line corporate boards is beyond me. It seems likely, though, that big checks from Hollywood donors have played a far bigger role than any allegiance to the First Amendment. The entertainment industry has given $125 million to Democrats since 1990, or about eight times as much money as the gun lobby gave to Republicans during the same period. In the 2004 election cycle, entertainment money going to Democrats outstripped gun money going to Republicans by a 30-to-1 ratio. Such money also easily beat out donations to the GOP by commercial banks and pharmaceutical companies.[7]

Democrats who cross Hollywood run the risk that this money might stop flowing. In 2000, when Joe Lieberman was on the presidential ticket—running with Tipper Gore's husband, no less—screenwriter Joe Eszterhas took out a full-page ad in *Variety* urging his industry friends not to open their checkbooks for the campaign. "Why should we in Hollywood vote or donate money to a man who threatens our creative freedom, our freedom of expression?" Eszterhas asked. In this case, nobody listened. Al Gore was tight with the likes of Jeff Katzenberg and David Geffen, while Bill Clinton was worshipped by most of Malibu. The Hollywood money kept coming in 2000, but the threat of a dry spigot is always there.[8]

Beyond money, there is a strong cultural affinity between the elites who run the Democratic Party and those who set the tone in Hollywood. Both these groups are much more secular than most of America, and both are deeply committed to the social gains of the past half century. Modern liberalism owes a huge debt to the entertainment industry for helping change popular mores—whether by normalizing working women through sitcoms such as *The Mary Tyler Moore Show*, or introducing gay characters in shows such as *Ellen* to mainstream America, or using movies and television to spotlight social problems, from AIDS to racism. A single movie like *Brokeback Mountain* can do more to change attitudes than a hundred grassroots campaigns. Maybe the left doesn't control any of the three branches of government, but at least it has DreamWorks.

While the liberal love affair with Hollywood is easy to understand, its effect is to narrow the debate over what's wrong with the mass media or what to do about it. We hear about Janet Jackson's breast for two weeks—and nothing about the perversity of *My Super Sweet Sixteen*. A few explicit sex scenes in *Grand Theft Auto: San Andreas* provoke a firestorm, even as we grow inured to the fact that much "news" these days seems to be about white women missing in the Caribbean or murdered by their husbands. Meanwhile, the roots of our rotten popular culture— near-total private control of all media—are seldom attacked. They are rarely even discussed.

IF YOU'RE MY AGE, you have fond memories of watching television as a kid. Maybe you remember learning a thing or two about shoe phones on *Get Smart*. Or perhaps you took some lessons in wheeling and dealing from Danny Partridge. You might have had a television in your room, but it probably didn't get many channels. You might have had an Atari video game, where you could blast away at crude digital blobs posing as Space Invaders.

How quaint all this seems today.

There are no parallels in history, recent or distant, to how much media kids are exposed to in this country. No society has ceded so much power over the values of its youth so rapidly as America has in the past few decades— and the last few years in particular.

I will get to hard facts in a moment, but first meet my ten-year-old niece, Perry. She is a great kid and she already has quite the reputation for being precociously good at connecting with people in a kind and considerate way. She has been raised right and has excellent values, to the extent such qualities are visible in a ten-year-old.

I can only hope Perry stays this way. The other night I was having dinner with her, her father, and my parents. The television is never on during meals at Perry's house, which puts her household in the minority. But Perry was distracted anyway, because next to her dinner plate she had a small electronic toy the size of a stopwatch. Every few minutes, the thing would emit a beep and Perry would snatch it up, study it, and press a few buttons. This game went on through dinner, and I still can't figure out exactly what she was playing—but then, the vast universe of hand-held video games is mostly a black hole to my generation. Over forty million handheld video games were sold in 2004 alone, totaling a billion dollar in sales. In contrast, nearly 70 percent of households did not purchase a single book for someone under fourteen in 2003. Kids everywhere are glued to these gizmos—some of which can play movies and music, take pictures, and make phone calls.[9]

Perry has plenty of books and she's a good reader. But after she excused herself from the table that night, she also had the choice of watching television alone in her room. And like many kids, her color television is hooked up to cable and has a remote control. Perry used to just watch cartoon channels, but she's getting older now, becoming a "tweener," and cartoons don't have the allure they once did. Her father sets rules on what she can watch, but while the adults finished dinner, it is hard to say for sure what Perry might have stumbled across during those early prime-time hours. I do know that she has about sixty-five channels, and that anytime I cruise through these same channels I invariably see something violent and disturbing, or something sexual and titillating, or something so stupid that I fear for my IQ if I linger too long—something like the frequent E! rerun, *101 Sexiest Celebrity Bodies*.

Chances are that Perry will be just fine no matter how much channel surfing she does as she grows up. After all, I watched a few hundred episodes of *Starsky & Hutch* and I turned out okay (I think). Yet there is enough alarming research out there that I do not take Perry's future well-being for granted.

Start with the basic facts about kids and media exposure. "Young people in the U.S. inhabit an environment that is not just media rich—it is media saturated," stated a major study of kids and media conducted in 2004 by the Kaiser Family Foundation. Recent years have seen an explosion in the amount of media technology in the hands of a typical kid. More than two-thirds of young people ages eight to eighteen now have a TV in their room, over half have a VCR, and half have their own video game console. Over a third of kids get cable or satellite channels in their room, including premium channels like HBO. Many kids also have their own computers, although only one-fifth can jump on the web in their rooms—a percentage sure to rise rapidly as broadband and wireless spread.[10]

Whatever media a kid doesn't have are nearly always available elsewhere in the house: Over 80 percent of households with children now get cable or satellite channels, two-thirds are connected to the Internet, and 85 percent have video game consoles. Meanwhile, about 40 percent of kids have their own cell phones, including over a third of eleven- to fourteen-year olds; more than half have handheld video games, and the vast majority have a portable music player. Kids are even getting BlackBerries.

In all, children today have access to far more media than they did when I was growing up—and far more than was available even five years ago. Another thing that seems to have changed is what researchers call "household TV orientation"—that is, the attitude of parents toward television, as well as toward other media. Parents don't talk much these days about "the plug-in drug" or "the idiot box." They're often as glued to the television as their kids are. The Kaiser study found that over half of youths live in households where the TV is on constantly, even when no one is watching, and nearly two thirds live in homes where the TV is *"usually on" during meals*. In addition, the study found that 53 percent of kids report living in homes where there are no rules about television. Nor do many parents lay down the law when it comes to the content of Internet or video games or music.[11]

In short, most kids can imbibe any media they want as much as they want—including the same content available to adults. And, boy, do they want it: On average kids spend more than four hours a day watching TV and videos, nearly two hours listening to music (mostly hip-hop), and about an hour playing video games. In contrast, the daily dose of reading for kids is about forty-five minutes, while average homework time clocks in at just under an hour. Meanwhile, kids are just a few clicks away from thousands of porn sites.[12]

There has also been a trend toward more media in the lives of very young children. Most parents don't have a clue that the American Academy of Pediatrics recommends that children under two not be exposed to *any* screen media. What they do know is that television feels like a gift from heaven when raising kids, especially for burned-out working parents who can't bear the thought of reading *Curious*

George Flies a Kite for the twenty-sixth time after a long day at the office. One study found that 59 percent of children under two watch over two hours a day of television or videos, and that 30 percent of children under a year to age three have a television in their room. (At what point toddlers develop the digital dexterity to work a remote control is unclear.)[13]

Recently, at a dinner party, I heard two parents discussing what their five-year-old son should watch in the bedroom while the adults ate. "Anything but the Cartoon Network!" the wife shouted after her husband as the boy was hauled off to be pacified by a twenty-three-inch screen. And that is what television has come to. Even the cartoons—*especially* the cartoons—are risky fare.

The National Television Violence Study published in 1998 remains the largest content analysis of television ever undertaken. For three years, researchers watched almost 10,000 hours of broadcast and cable programs randomly selected from twenty-three channels. What they found is that nearly two out of three television programs included some violence, with an average of six violent acts per hour. Violence was also found to be prevalent in 68 percent of children's programs, and a typical hour of such programs contained fourteen violent incidents. A child who watches two hours of cartoons a day sees nearly 10,000 violent incidents *each year*. Only the slimmest fraction of shows with violence contained an antiviolence message of any kind.[14]

Maybe all this violence is harmless fun, as some insist. Maybe it is even a necessary form of catharsis for kids, a healthy emotional outlet as Gerard Jones has argued in his book *Killing Monsters: Why Children Need Fantasy, Super-Heroes, and Make-Believe Violence.* Or maybe violent shows and video games actually make people smarter, as writer Steven Johnson suggests in his book *Everything Bad Is Good for You.* Maybe a twelve-year-old who learns how to follow the complex murder investigations on *CSI* is pushing his growing brain to work a lot harder, to the point that the SATs will be a cinch later on. (Why didn't Princeton Review think of this?)

Or maybe not.

A QUICK STORY BEFORE getting to the research. In the early 1970s, my great hero in life was Billy Jack. This part-Indian savior of a hippie school in New Mexico was the very embodiment of righteous violence, and it was impossible to feel even the slightest sympathy for the rednecks that he dispatched with roundhouse kicks. At the age of eight, I saw the original *Billy Jack* three times and the next year, 1974, I saw *The Return of Billy Jack* four times. Among other things, these movies included the vicious rape of a schoolteacher and the sadistic police beating of a teenager. How I got into these disturbing movies so young I do not know.

Watching *Billy Jack* as an adult, I now understand that

the guy had a serious anger management problem, to put things charitably. But as a kid I thought he was infallible and possibly the answer to America's problems. As I sported my BILLY JACK FOR PRESIDENT button, the only question I had was, how can I be like Billy Jack?

My chance to be like Billy came one day after school in second grade. I had a classmate who vaguely bothered me, and so I decided he would be the perfect guinea pig on which to try out a karate kick. In one scene in *Billy Jack*, a barefoot Billy tells the evil sheriff, Posner: "I'm going to take my right foot and put it across your left cheek, and there is not a thing you can do to stop me." I wanted to do the same move on my classmate, so I confronted the poor kid on his way home from school, and as other kids egged me on, I made a big to-do of slowly taking off my shoes, just like Billy did before every fight. My victim was petrified, and fortunately for both of us he made a narrow escape before I could do anything involving his left cheek or my right foot.

This is a small and amusing story, and literally child's play compared to, say, the dozen-plus murders that have reportedly been inspired by Oliver Stone's movie *Natural Born Killers*. I tell it only because I think of Billy Jack every time I read yet another study about the link between real and make-believe aggression. Given my own experience, however mild, such a link has always struck me as obvious, and now there is more research than ever to support that intuition.

Armies of researchers, laboring over decades, have documented three kinds of bad effects that watching violence can have on viewers: making them more prone to aggressive behavior, desensitizing them to violence or lowering empathy, and leading them to develop irrational fears of being the victim of violence. Certainly, in our bloody, cold-hearted, and distrusting society, there are plenty of people exhibiting all three traits, but can anyone say for sure that the media are even partly to blame for this? Studies have explored the matter of causation in several ways, including through controlled experiments. One study in the 1990s compared a group of kids in a classroom who had watched a single episode of *Mighty Morphin' Power Rangers* to another group who hadn't seen the episode. In the classroom where the show had been watched, viewers engaged in seven times as many aggressive acts toward each other, such as hitting and shoving, as the kids who hadn't seen the show. Additional experiments found that watching *Mister Rogers' Neighborhood* led kids to act cooperatively and share their toys, while episode of *Batman* and *Spiderman* produced more hostile behavior.[15]

In recent years, researchers have also documented how video games and music make kids aggressive. A 2003 study—not unique by any means—found that violent music led to more hostile thoughts and aggressive actions among five hundred college students. The researchers observed: "There are now good theoretical and empirical reasons to expect effects of music lyrics on aggressive behavior to be similar to the well studied effects of exposure to TV and movie violence." The verdict is largely the same on video games, annual sales of which have surpassed movie box-office receipts. New technologies have made these games, most of which contain some violent content, far more realistic. While the games are now rated like movies, this doesn't stop 87 percent of all U.S. preteen and teenage boys from playing "M-rated" games (M is for Mature).[16]

"Whoever tells the stories defines the culture," commented one team of academics who studied video games. "What do we think the effect is when our kids' storytellers are violence simulators that glorify gang culture, celebrate brutality, lionize crudeness, and trivialize violence toward women?"[17]

The answer to this question is increasingly clear. A 2001 research overview found that "across 54 independent tests of the relations between video game violence and aggression, involving 4,262 participants, there appear to be five consistent results of playing games with violent content. Playing video games increases aggressive behaviors, increases aggressive cognition, increases aggressive emotions, increases physiological arousal, and decreases prosocial behaviors."[18] Of course, it's not just kids who play these games. A lot of adults do, too. And while violent crime is way down, media fare of this sort may help explain why the word "rage" has become a suffix. We now have not only road rage, but air rage, office rage, phone rage, and store rage. Scholar Jessie Klein has called America a "bully society," citing the myriad ways in which people push each other around in daily life.

While there have been hundreds of research studies positing a link between violence and media, plenty of skeptics remain, and they have actually grown louder. One study found that as the evidence of such a link has grown more damning, "news reports about the effects of media violence have shifted to weaker statements, implying that there is little evidence for such effects."[19] This trend extends to public intellectuals who should know better—perhaps because there is such a premium placed on clever, counterintuitive thinking. You don't make a name for yourself these days by echoing decades of research. You win accolades by arguing that what we all know to be true isn't, that wrong is right, or black is white, or that "everything bad is good for you." Author Steven Johnson was widely praised for taking on the conventional wisdom that media makes us dumber. But few critics seemed to notice that he barely mentioned the chief complaint about media these days, which is not that it makes us stupid, but that it pollutes our culture and undermines the values most people embrace and wish to pass down to their children.

Americans say it is mainly the responsibility of parents to shield kids from inappropriate media. Parents aren't doing that very well, nor do those who want to do a better job get much help. As you'll notice from picking up your remote control or visiting Blockbuster, the good stuff is a smaller and smaller portion of the overall media on-slaught, especially on television. The oases of smart pro-gramming are lost in what President Kennedy's FCC chairman once called "a vast wasteland." Even the once in-telligent channels on cable, such as Discovery, A&E, and the History Channel, are turning sensationalistic to boost ratings. Or there's Oxygen, which started out as a high-minded venture only to end up in a gutter of sex-and-murder true-crime.

Likewise, insipid music is more dominant—perhaps because 90 percent of music production is controlled by only five corporations and control over the outlets for this music is even more monopolistic. Clear Channel increas-ingly decides what music Americans hear through its ownership of 1,200 radio stations, as well as SFX Enter-tainment, America's largest concert-venue owner and tour promoter. Independent record stores are disappearing, re-placed by a few large retailers. In some areas, Wal-Mart is the only place to buy CDs. Online music offers plenty of alternatives—assuming you have any way of hearing about them. As for magazines, most young people in America don't do a lot of reading, even when their ADD medication is working. Kids report spending just thirteen minutes a day with magazines, and those who do read nearly always go for publications such as *Teen People* and *YM*, which are owned by a few corporate conglomerates.[20]

Meanwhile, the other core dimension of media in America—advertising—is becoming more ubiquitous and invasive, especially in the lives of children. It has been estimated that total advertising and marketing expenditures aimed at children reached $15 billion in 2004, up from $100 million in television advertising spent in 1983. The average American kid sees 40,000 commercials a year. Kids are also increasingly exposed to advertising at school and in other places, such as summer camp. As Juliet Schor has written, marketing is "fundamentally altering the experience of childhood. Corporations have infiltrated the core activities and institutions of childhood, with virtually no resistance from government or parents."[21]

Add up all the mass media that now saturate the lives of kids and the bottom line is this: Parents, schools, and churches are fast losing their power to shape the values of the next generations. Instead, that power is being ceded to private actors who are motivated mainly by financial self-interest. Is that who should be teaching our children? I don't think so.

Strangely, though, even as the case for noncommercial media grows more urgent, the alternatives we do have are coming under siege.

Take the attack on public broadcasting. The Public Broadcasting Act of 1967 was signed by President Johnson with the goal of fostering noncommercial television and radio, and it has been a huge success. The Corporation for Public Broadcasting supported 270 public radio and television stations in 1969. By 2003, that number had grown to 1,100, and these stations reach the vast majority of American households with a wide of variety of programming, from hallowed children's shows such as *Sesame Street* to eclectic radio programs such as *Car Talk* to news shows such as *The NewsHour with Jim Lehrer* and *All Things Considered*. The annual cost to taxpayers of all this good stuff is just over $400 million a year—less than what we spend annually to subsidize peanut growers. These federal dollars, in turn, help leverage another $1.9 billion every year from other sources, including individuals and businesses, in a classic case of government "steering, not rowing."

What's not to like about public broadcasting?

Nothing, if you ask ordinary Americans. Even Mother Teresa never had approval ratings as high as PBS. One national survey in 2003 found that 90 percent of Americans saw PBS as "a valuable cultural resource," 89 percent believed it "provides high-quality programming," 80 percent agreed that its "programs reflect the diversity and character of America," and 92 percent agreed that "PBS is a safe place for children to watch television because of its nonviolent, educational, commercial-free programming."[22]

With poll numbers like these, you'd think politicians would compete to throw money at public broadcasting. You'd think that the more Americans fretted about *Growing Up Gotti*, the more generous Congress would be to *Sesame Street*. You might even imagine that the Republican Party, which complains most about Hollywood's subversion of family values, would be PBS's biggest fan, and that by now Karl Rove would have found a way to make Big Bird a GOP icon.

If you thought these things, you'd obviously be from another country. Public broadcasting is like national health insurance: People in other wealthy countries take it for granted, while here politicians see it as evil. Nixon tried to kill public broadcasting. Reagan tried. Newt Gingrich tried. And now Congress is trying again. In June 2005, the House Appropriations Committee whacked the Corporation for Public Broadcasting's budget nearly in half, and though some of this money was restored, more attacks are coming.

Critics offer a number of reasons for going after public broadcasting, including the budget crunch and the purported liberal bias of NPR and PBS. The latter claim doesn't ring true to most viewers: 80 percent of Americans say they consider the programming on PBS and NPR to be "fair and balanced," and are no more likely to think that PBS has a liberal bias than the major networks.[23] While PBS is famously home to Bill Moyers, it has also provided a platform over the years to such leading conservatives as William F. Buckley, Ben Wattenberg, and John McLaughlin. Most recently it gave a show to Tucker Carlson, who was already ubiquitous enough, thank you.

Anyway, only a fraction of the three thousand hours of PBS's annual programming could be considered controversial. A third of this content is for children, a third is historical or cultural, and a third is news and current affairs. According to PBS's president, only thirty hours of programming—or 1 percent—generated any controversy during 2003–2004. Presumably *Antiques Roadshow* was not on that list.[24]

The beef with public broadcasting goes much deeper than the matter of bias, of course. For critics there is a larger principle at stake, which is that the free market should be the sole provider of goods and services. If Americans really want to watch documentaries on the Civil War, or if they really want *This Old House*, then surely private media owners will cater to these needs. That's the way supply and demand works.

Or so the theory goes. Reality is another story. Despite persistent public complaints about the content of commercial media, television and movies have only grown more violent and sexual in recent decades. Nielsen ratings and box-office tallies may suggest that Americans "get what they want," flocking to some of the worst stuff that Hollywood produces. It is also safe to say that gladiatorial contests at Yankee Stadium would be sold out. And who knows, maybe the recent advent of pay-per-view "extreme fighting" is a prelude to the Colosseum's return.

Whatever they watch, many Americans grasp that the clamor for ratings and advertising dollars leads the media to fan people's basest instincts. Amid such a descent, only the most rigid ideologues could conclude that now is a good time to snuff out America's popular alternative to commercial broadcasting. And only ideologues—or bribed politicians—would dare go even farther, trying to do away entirely with public regulation of the media.

Attacks on government oversight of the media are a longstanding hobby in Washington. These attacks have been so successful that many Americans don't know how much power the federal government once had—and still does have on paper—over broadcast media. A key feature of the Federal Communications Act of 1934 was the notion of a quid pro quo between broadcasters and viewers. Private broadcasters would get access to the airwaves—a resource owned by all Americans—and in return they would have to serve the public interest. Simple enough.

Then along came decades of industry pressure and campaign money to steadily erode the concept that corporations owed anything to anyone in return for broadcasting rights. Over time, even the most basic efforts to regulate content in the public interest became more difficult. So, for example, in 1974 the Federal Communications Commission cracked down on advertisers' manipulation of children by imposing limits on how many ads could be shown per hour and mandating clearer distinctions between ads and programs. While these rules were seen as half measures by media watchdogs of that time, the industry saw them as intolerable, and in 1981 the Reagan administration succeeded in sharply curtailing the FCC's role.

Now and again the zeal for regulation resurfaces in atrophied form. In 1990, after years of growing cartoon nastiness, Congress passed the Children's Television Act, which requires that television stations carry three hours a week of educational programming. Even these paltry requirements are not fully enforced, however.

With efforts to regulate content off the table, in the 1990s politicians in Washington grew fond of demanding "voluntary" ratings for all sorts of media, and the entertainment industry largely went along with such demands. These ratings were supposed to work in tandem with the V-chips installed by law in all new televisions, and with active monitoring by parents. The result? As of 2004, only about 15 percent of parents said they had ever used the V-chip, while only one in four said they "often" use TV ratings to guide their kids' choices. Many parents say they have no clue whether their TV even has a V-chip and, anyway, they find the various ratings to be indecipherable.[25] Worse, some researchers have suggested that the ratings steer younger viewers toward more adult content—serving as ads, in effect, for forbidden fruit.[26]

Could today's cultural pollution get even worse? You bet. Eventually we'll see the convergence of television and the Internet, which will bring an avalanche of new content to the small screen and make it even harder to find the good stuff or weed out the bad. And even as the Internet becomes the conduit of all media, it may become less open and more beholden to private interests. Already, major telecom companies insist that they can use their domination of broadband services to decide what consumers can access on the Internet. These monopolistic practices have been endorsed by the FCC and by the Supreme Court in the notorious *Brand X* decision. While it's hard to imagine that a few big companies could wield even more influence over popular culture and social values than they do now, this is exactly where we are headed.

Then there is the rise of virtual reality media. In his 2005 book *Synthetic Worlds*, Edward Castronova suggests that we may not be far from a time when simulated reality is more attractive to many people than real life. Already a fair number of Americans spend more much time immersed in electronic make-believe realms than they spend with friends or partners. Today, kids sit in the backseat of the family SUV with an iPod in their ears and a Game Boy in their hands. Tomorrow they'll be wearing virtual reality goggles—already available in primitive form—sealed off not just from their parents, but from the real world. The companies that design the alternate universes these kids inhabit will have growing influence over what they believe and value—more influence, in many cases, than the flesh-and-blood up in the front seat.

Elements of this disembodied future are already here. The "human moment" is in rapid decline. People see, touch, and speak to each other less—e-mailing co-workers all day who sit ten feet away, or text-messaging a lover instead of calling, or doing all their shopping not with the help of a clerk but with the click of a mouse. Whole romances start and end online. Legions of workers have employers they have never met. Students in "distance learning" programs have professors they will never see. More family time is spent in front of separate screens, in separate rooms. We may look back not long from now and think nostalgically about how close families once were—back when they watched television together during meals.

Maybe none of this matters. The truth is that we don't know what will be the long-term effects of separating people from one another and substituting human contact with a growing diet of interactive media. Optimists project new forms of virtual community, and we can see a lot of this already. Being a gay teenager in Montana has never been less lonely. Judging from experience so far, though, it's likely that the bigger shift will be toward ever more extreme forms of individualism—much of it channeled in ways that benefit someone's bottom line.

CENSORSHIP IS NOT the solution to this mess. For one thing, it would be ineffective in an age of proliferating media outlets. Policing a handful of networks is hard. Policing two hundred channels on DishTV would be harder. Patrolling a virtual universe of eight billion web pages is impossible.

Censorship is also at odds with American ideals of freedom. While some controls on media content, such as ratings, V-chip technology, and basic obscenity rules around broadcasting, make sense, a deeper government role in regulating content would be a scary thing. There is too much potential for regulators to impose their particular morality on everyone else, or to kowtow to certain religious groups, or to use censorship to prop up the powers that be. Censorship that went far enough to make a real impact on the cultural climate wouldn't just alarm liberals; populists and libertarians, already deeply distrustful of the feds, would also revolt.

So forget the debate about censorship. It's a dead end, except if you work in the fundraising department of the ACLU or Focus on the Family.

What *is* the solution? We need a new vision of media reform that embraces freedom of speech but also demands responsibility, both from individuals and from society at large. Here, as elsewhere, defending core American values means changing behavior while confronting the market forces that work against those values.

Three strategies come to mind.

First, we need to reregulate broadcasting. Any private entity that uses the airwaves *we all own* should be held accountable to the public interest. To figure out what this means, just dust off definitions from the 1960s and '70s, formulated by regulators from both parties of educational programming, advertising standards, and quality news. Or, look to more recent work that outlines how broadcasters could serve the public interest around election time with free airtime for candidates and more televised debates. The ideas are out there; what has been missing is political will. Media reformers try to build such will by invoking the specter of corporate control and diminished democracy. That's one way to go. A better way is to tap into public anxiety about values and advance a moral rationale for media regulation. After all, the ominous political clout of Viacom or Disney is hard to grasp, while the junk they peddle is in our face every day.

Second, we need more alternatives to for-profit media and arts. Government funds go a long way here, by leveraging other money. So let's spend more. A lot more. We can finance this spending by earmarking part of the revenues generated by auctioning the digital broadcasting spectrum. That money—billions of dollars—will become available as America makes the transition from analog to digital broadcasting over the coming years. Let's grab some of it and set up an independent trust for public broadcasting that is beyond the reach of budget cutters. More money for the arts is a perennial item on the liberal wish list, and maintaining current funding levels is hard enough these days. But the dynamics of this issue could shift if greater public funding for media and culture were sold as part of a larger call to moral renewal.

A third strategy is to change people's behavior. It's no good to have better media choices if parents keep the TV on during dinner or let their kids have one hundred channels in their bedroom or put violent Xbox games like *Fight Night* 3 under the Christmas tree. Thirty years ago a critical stance toward media and advertising was part of the popular consciousness. Public intellectuals, elected leaders, and regulators helped create that awareness— mainstreaming concepts like "subliminal advertising," and they can do it again. Books such as *No Logo* by Naomi Klein and *Born to Buy* by Juliet Schor have begun this work. Many advocacy groups are also sounding the alarm about media content, especially violent content. Some liberal faith groups are raising these concerns, too, and civil society groups have a crucial role to play here. But where are the politicians? They're mostly on the right, that's where—typically advocating censorship. And censorship is exactly what we may get if leaders on the left and in the center don't speak up.

If that means pissing off West Coast big shots, fine. Democrats need to do the right thing, and heartland votes are more important than Hollywood dollars.

CHAPTER FIVE

Punishment for Some

O N MARCH 12, 2000, A MAN NAMED GARY EWING entered the pro shop of the El Segundo Golf Course in Los Angeles County. When he left, a clerk noticed that he was walking with an odd limp, as if he were concealing something. The employee called the police, who arrived in time to confront Ewing in the parking lot. The cops found three Callaway golf clubs shoved down his pants leg, and Ewing was arrested for shoplifting.

Only ten months earlier, Ewing had been paroled from prison after serving six years for a series of burglaries, including one in which he had threatened someone with a knife. Ewing was a crack user back then, and he had been stealing most of his adult life. He was first arrested for theft in 1984 when he was twenty-two. In 1988 he was busted for stealing a car. There were other arrests, too, although none for serious violent crimes. Somewhere along the line, Ewing contracted AIDS. The disease had already blinded him in one eye. After he was paroled, an assortment of medications kept Ewing alive as he eked out an existence on the margins of society.

If Ewing didn't live in California, or had committed his theft a half decade earlier, his crime at the golf course might have sent him back to prison for a few more years. Instead, thanks to the three strikes law that California adopted in 1994, he was sentenced to twenty-five years. Given his poor health, this amounted to a life sentence.

In December 2005, as Ewing served his fifth year for shoplifting, justice was done in another crime involving golf. This one involved a Utah real-estate developer named Angelo Degenhardt. In the late 1990s, Degenhardt had raised millions of dollars from investors to build a golf resort in Midvale, in the Salt Lake Valley. Such resorts are something of a craze these days and epitomize a certain image of the good life: luxury hotel accommodations just steps away from the green. Developers can make big profits building golf resorts, and so can their investors— assuming they are dealing with someone honest. But Degenhardt wasn't honest, prosecutors would later say, and his company allegedly defrauded investors of more than $4 million.

One woman had put money saved for graduate school into Degenhardt's golf resort, since it seemed like a sure way to get ahead, only to find her finances wiped out. She had to abandon her dream of becoming a physical therapist. A golf professional left a good job to join with Degenhardt, investing $120,000. The move destroyed his career. Construction on the golf resort never even started.

Financial frauds are extremely common these days. Succeeding in business without really trying has always been an American ideal, and today hopes for easy money burn hotter than ever, thanks to a stock bubble followed by a real-estate boom, as well as constant news reports of nobodies who struck it rich with some obscure patent or brainless franchise. The key to wealth, it might seem, is not working hard so much as pushing the right buttons, and nearly every part of the business world has a gray zone populated by shady characters in search of shortcuts. Lax regulation ensures a Wild West mentality in some industries, real estate among them. Local and state law enforcement agencies are so overwhelmed with reports of fraud that many don't even bother with cases involving less than $100,000. And even the big cases can be very hard to prove beyond a reasonable doubt—a fact that fraudsters well know.

Degenhardt was indicted in 2003 for the golf course scam, and authorities worked hard to build a strong case against him. They didn't have much luck. Degenhardt's lawyers fought the charges for several years before exhausted prosecutors finally agreed to a plea bargain. Degenhardt copped to one felony count of securities fraud. His punishment? Six months' home confinement, along with restitution to his victims.

When Degenhardt was sentenced, the prosecutor in the case said that "lives have been wrecked" by his crime. The light sentence, however, "is justice as best as it can get under the circumstances." Degenhardt is supposed to pay back his victims $3,840,500, but according to a court order, he needn't pay more than $500 a month.[1]

At that rate, Degenhardt will be all paid up in about six hundred years.

No job is more important for government than keeping its citizens safe. Among other things, this means protecting people from traditional forms of street crime, like violence and theft, as well as from other threats—including killer consumer products, deadly work conditions, and financial frauds. In a liberal republic, we all get freedom but have an obligation to refrain from harming or controlling any other person. Guys like Degenhardt shouldn't be allowed to treat your nest egg as their ticket to easy luxury, just as someone like Gary Ewing shouldn't be able finance his drug habit off the stolen merchandise from your shop.

Street crime gets all the attention because these crimes are scarier and affect people's daily habits more, such as walking the streets at night. On the other hand, white-collar criminals steal far larger sums and seriously imperil our health and safety. Liberals have a mixed record of stopping street crime, while conservatives have shown little interest in thwarting "suite crime." Predictably, though, only liberals have been tagged as "soft on crime." This reputation has been devastating in the broader debate over values. If liberals can't stand up to even the most dangerous forms of personal irresponsibility, how can they be expected to promote moral order anywhere else?

What is typically missing from this conversation, however, is the basic truth that high crime rates are endemic to the American experience and to our rough-and-tumble brand of capitalism. This is a nation that has always been more focused on the ends than the means, and some of the very qualities that produce success in the United States, such as risk taking and irreverence toward authority, are conducive to a criminal mind-set. Also, the universalist ideal of America—the notion that everyone can get rich— raises wide hopes for the good life that can lead to crime when legitimate means of upward mobility don't work out. As the sociologist Robert Merton once wrote, the "moral mandate" to get ahead in America "exerts pressure to succeed, by fair means if possible and by foul means if necessary." Another study put the problem this way: "If Americans are exceptionally resistant to social control—and therefore exceptionally vulnerable to criminal temptations—it is because they live in a society that enshrines the unfettered pursuit of individual material success above all other values."[2]

The United States has always had much higher violent crime rates than other Western countries. America's cities were famously violent through much of the nineteenth century (think *Gangs of New York*) as was the frontier. Organized crime and government graft were key paths upward for immigrant groups. These newcomers embraced the American ethos of achievement and financial success but lacked mainstream opportunities. So they got creative. Just because you didn't speak enough English to be a bank clerk or a bartender didn't mean you couldn't go into loan sharking or bootlegging.[3] And once your ethnic group got its turn to loot government, the real cash would roll in. The great historian James Truslow Adams commented in 1928 that America is "the most lawless in spirit of any of the great modern civilized countries. Lawlessness has been and is one of the most distinctive American traits. . . . It is needless to say that we are not going to be able to shed this heritage quickly or easily." Adams made this remark at the height of a crime wave during the Roaring Twenties that rivaled the mayhem of the 1980s crack epidemic.[4]

The close link between crime and the populist ideals of American capitalism raises doubts about both liberal and conservative solutions to crime. Conservatives tend to link high crime rates to a moral breakdown and obsession with rights that began in the 1960s, ignoring the fact that America was famous for crime long before *Miranda* and welfare moms came along. Liberals tend to think that poverty is the cause of crime. So why did crime fall during the Great Depression and go up in the prosperous decades after World War II? The unpleasant truth is that increased opportunity may actually abet crime by whetting more appetites for wealth. Also, the liberal view doesn't account for white collar crime, which is often committed by people who have plenty of money already.

Adams was right when he noted, more than seventy-five years ago, that it won't be easy for America to overcome its heritage of crime. Even as the mass incarceration of recent years (among other factors) has helped reduce street crime, there are plenty of signs that white-collar crime is getting worse. This would make sense, given the direction of American society. Those strains of the national culture that foster criminality have been growing, not decreasing. We live at a time when financial success is increasingly equated with personal virtue. Nearly all of our role models these days are wealthy. And as the "moral mandate" to succeed grows ever more intense, the bar is getting higher in terms of what it costs to enjoy a middle-class life, much less be "rich." The point is not that there isn't opportunity in America; there is, and even half-wit real-estate agents can make six figures. The point is that no matter how much opportunity exists, there is never enough to go around in a society where most income gains go to the top 20 percent of households—even as we are all told that we can get rich and our noses are pushed up against the glass of affluent lifestyles. Meanwhile, harsh competition is promoted nightly on reality TV shows as a natural thing. The message is that we must rely on ourselves, and that no one will—or should—catch us if we fall.

A certain kind of desperation drives America. And there's no denying that this trait helps account for the incredible vitality of our society, as well as an economy that produces no end of innovative products and first-rate services. There's also no denying that the desperation has drawbacks. If it's every man for himself, why not do whatever it takes to get ahead? If self-interest is such a great virtue and people step on each other legally all the time, how immoral can it be to step on someone *illegally?* Here, as elsewhere, we haven't figured out how to balance freedom and responsibility. America's current brand of economic freedom yields all the good things that come from dynamic competition, but nowadays business can be a lot like hockey—a game where there are no incentives to play nice and plenty of rewards if you get nasty.

Post-Enron, you would think that we'd all be more hip to the moral downsides of America's laissez-faire drift, but somehow this isn't the case. Insiders stole tens of billions of dollars from ordinary investors during the 1990s, abetted by corrupt politicians and sleeping watchdogs, and yet the scandals didn't produce much change beyond the Sarbanes-Oxley Act of 2002. Certainly there were no repercussions at the polls. A few of the leading bad guys, like WorldCom's Bernie Ebbers, got slammed with long prison terms. Most other wrongdoers—the Wall Street analysts who peddled junk stock or the lawyers who devised the fraudulent deals—never saw the inside of a courtroom, much less a prison cell.

A big problem is that Americans don't have any place to "put" the endless stories about white-collar crime. We have a clear narrative about how street crime reflects a collapse of personal responsibility—courtesy of the social freedoms brought to us by liberals. We don't have a narrative about how too much economic freedom leads to bad behavior. No matter how many executives we see in handcuffs, these images never quite add up to a popular appreciation of the obvious moral downsides of present-day capitalism. Nor do they add up to a public insistence that authorities go after street criminals and suite criminals with equal zeal, protecting us from both forms of predation.

The narrow ways in which we process crime were on vivid display in the aftermath of Hurricane Katrina. The media dwelled obsessively on shocking tales of rape and terror in the Superdome and convention center—reports that later turned out to be false. Images of looters wading through floodwaters with stolen microwaves and cartons of cigarettes were replayed again and again, especially on Fox News. Later there would be lurid tales of how displaced hurricane survivors spread mayhem wherever they went.

All this went effortlessly into the crime file that many Americans carry around in their heads. Urban black criminals, check. White victims, check. Poor people out of control, check. When William Bennett apologized for saying—not long after Katrina—that aborting every black baby in America would reduce crime, he explained himself by telling ABC News, "There was a lot of discussion about race and crime in New Orleans." The connections here aren't as much an analysis as a reflex.

Far harder to process have been the staggering financial crimes that followed Katrina. We don't have a file folder for these crimes, so mostly they end up in the mental wastebasket. Post-Katrina financial crimes fit into seven different categories. First: *energy price gouging.* A widespread problem after the storm, the gouging eventually resulted in fines in three states and a Congressional investigation of the major oil companies. Second: *insurance fraud.* This is an old story in the hurricane belt and part of a broader national problem. Property/casualty insurance fraud costs totaled $30 billion in 2004, according to the Insurance Information Institute.[5] That number will be much higher in

2005 thanks to Katrina. Third: *charity scams*. So many of these were reported after Katrina, some involving fake Web sites, that both the FBI and the IRS issued special warnings to the American public. Fourth: *FEMA fraud*. As in the aftermath of other hurricanes, FEMA found itself dealing with an avalanche of false claims. Nearly every day, for months after the storm, authorities in the Gulf states reported another arrest or indictment for defrauding FEMA. Fifth: *procurement fraud*. These frauds have involved overcharging government agencies for disaster-related rebuilding projects. Sixth: *false accounting*. Katrina provided convenient cover for some companies to make their earnings look better—and hence help stock value—by attributing losses to the hurricane that were caused by other factors. Seven: *Auto scams*. Over a quarter-million vehicles were damaged by Katrina, and most consumers would want to know if the used car they were about to buy had once been under water. However, through "title washing," in which a car's records are doctored, many salvage vehicles are now turning up at used-car dealers with no such warning.

What many of the Katrina scams have in common is that they were committed by fairly sophisticated people—in a lot of cases by people who are not career criminals but rather homeowners, businessmen, or other professionals, groups that tend to be disproportionately white and middle class. And we're not talking about everyday financial crimes here; these acts were committed in the wake of the greatest natural disaster ever to befall the United States. At a moment when all Americans should have been pulling together and making sacrifices, criminal self-interest thrived on a scale too large to track, much less prosecute.

Be that as it may, the popular memory about crime and Katrina still returns—by reflex—to unfounded stories about gang shootouts in the Superdome. The hurricane has done wonders for gun dealers in the half dozen states within easy driving distance of New Orleans. But has it helped pass federal legislation that would crack down on energy gouging? No. Has it led to a new push by federal and state authorities against insurance fraud? No. Has it prompted major new investigations of the questionable ways in which even legitimate charities raise and spend money? No. Has it resulted in any serious attempts to reduce the cronyism that surrounds federal contracts, whether in Baton Rouge or Baghdad? No.

The corporate scandals may have left barely a footprint on the public mind, but they at least yielded reforms. The crimes of Katrina have produced nothing.

PERSONAL RESPONSIBILITY is one of the great mantras of our time. This mantra has filled U.S. prisons to capacity, with over two million people now behind bars. It has led to "zero tolerance" policies in public schools, where eight-year-olds are getting arrested for classroom fights. The mantra cements mandatory drug sentences in place even as judges plead for flexibility and mothers plead for mercy. It keeps the executioners busy in Texas, where one or two people are now killed every month by lethal injection. America is hard on criminals as rarely before. It holds people accountable for their actions.

Or some people, anyway.

There have always been, and will always be, Americans of all classes who behave badly and pursue pleasure or self-interest in ways that hurt other citizens. The crimes of the lower classes are scarier; the crimes of the upper class are often more costly. We can quibble about which crimes deserve what punishment. We can argue about the mix of penal approaches that will best deter crimes and incapacitate or rehabilitate criminals. What we can't dispute—not in a democracy—is that justice should be applied equally across all groups.

Few contest this idea, at least openly. But as America has grown more economically stratified since the early 1970s, personal responsibility has been demanded in a more selective fashion. It has become not so much a serious moral principle as a political weapon. In his book *Punishment and Inequality in America,* the sociologist Bruce Western notes that "state power flows along the contours of social inequality," especially when it comes to crime and incarceration. It's no coincidence, he argues, that the "class inequalities in imprisonment increased as the economic status of low-education men deteriorated."[6]

This observation is not exactly astonishing; it seems intuitively obvious. Also intuitive is the other side of the coin: that as more money and power flows to the top of society, those in this strata won't be as subject to tough law enforcement. What good is a lot of clout, after all, if it doesn't translate into special treatment?

The facts bear out such intuition. Even as legislators have been busy imposing draconian standards of conduct on the poor over recent decades, they have been equally busy ensuring that the wealthy are held less accountable for their bad behavior. Look closely and you'll see two trend lines going in opposite directions: tougher laws and more prison cells to deal with street crime; looser regulations and fewer investigators to police white-collar crime.

A good place to pick up this part of the story is in Cincinnati, in June 2002. That month a young plumber's apprentice named Patrick Walters was buried alive in a ten-foot-deep trench. Walters was in the trench working on a sewer pipe when the walls of the trench, soaked through from recent rains, collapsed around him. The accident could easily have been avoided if Walters's employer had complied with federal safety laws and sent him into the trench with the protection of a steel box. But the employer, a firm called Moeves Plumbing, was known for flouting such laws. Just two weeks before Walters died, his throat filled with sludge, a safety investigator had found men from the same company working in an unprotected trench that was fifteen-feet deep. Walters himself had told the investigator about unsafe practices at the company and of his fears of being entombed. Thirteen years earlier, another worker from Moeves had died in a nearly identical fashion as Walters—buried in a deep trench when the walls collapsed. Following that tragedy, the company had paid a $13,000 fine and vowed to improve its safety procedures. That vow had been forgotten over the years, and even the company's "safety manager" admitted that he hadn't provided any safety training during his two years with Moeves.

It is a criminal offense to cause the death of a worker due to a willful disregard of safety rules, and the case against Moeves Plumbing was about as strong as they come. Walters's grieving family lobbied the federal agency that oversees workplace safety—the Occupational Safety and Health Administration—to refer the case to the Justice Department for prosecution. Their efforts included a direct appeal to John Henshaw, the OSHA administrator. Henshaw had been appointed to OSHA by President Bush, and even though his main qualification for the job was a background in corporate America, labor unions had viewed him as one of the president's better appointments. But by the time of Walters' death, Henshaw was in the second year of a rollback of workplace safety efforts. OSHA had already scrapped new rules—ten years in the making—aimed at protecting workers from repetitive strain injuries, which accounted for one third of all serious workplace injuries. It had also stopped work on dozens of other new safety measures, instead emphasizing toothless "voluntary programs" for enforcing safety rules. "The Bush Administration has the worst record on safety rules in OSHA's entire history," observed a leading labor union, in a claim echoed by others.[7]

John Henshaw had not been hired to protect workers from death or maiming; he had been hired to defend the business interests who helped elect George W. Bush. Henshaw declined to refer the Walters case for prosecution.

Instead, OSHA cited Moeves Plumbing for violations of safety rules. The company was fined $45,000, payable over four years. It was not forced to admit wrongdoing. Just two years later, in August 2004, OSHA inspectors visited a Moeves Plumbing job in Ohio and found employees working in a nine-foot trench that was dangerously exposed to cave-in. While Moeves had already killed two of its men over the years, they were apparently willing to sacrifice more. This time OSHA got really tough with Moeves. For its fifth violation of safety rules in a decade, the company was fined $150,000—again payable in installments.

The Moeves case fits into a familiar pattern. More than five thousand employees are killed annually on the job, about one hundred workers a week. Another sixty thousand die annually from occupational disease. And not a few of these deaths are akin to manslaughter. Between 1982 and 2002, according to a *New York Times* investigation, OSHA investigated 1,242 worker deaths that agency investigators blamed on "willful" safety violations—that is employers who knowingly created conditions where a worker might die, typically to save a few bucks. Yet the agency sought prosecution in only 7 percent of these cases. Many of the employers let off the hook went on to kill more workers. OSHA's reluctance to prosecute, the *Times* found, "persisted even when employers had been cited before for the very same safety violation. It persisted even when the violations caused multiple deaths, or when the victims were teenagers. And it persisted even where reviews by administrative judges found persistent proof of wrongdoing."[8]

Not that prosecution would have been a big deal. Under federal law, killing a worker through negligence is nothing more than a misdemeanor, and the maximum jail sentence is six months—less time than you might face for shoplifting. Eleven states have enacted stiffer penalties, but efforts to make causing a worker's death a federal felony have been repeatedly rejected by Congress—including by the same get-tough legislators who backed stiff mandatory minimum sentences for drug possession. Washington has also signaled what sort of personal responsibility really matters by depriving OSHA of the resources it needs to do its job.

OSHA was formed in 1970, and the agency is estimated to have saved the lives of more than 300,000 workers in the past thirty-five years. It has never been popular with business, since it's generally cheaper to let workers die now and again than to ensure their safety.[9]

As the Republican Party moved right, it declared open season on regulation and began an attack on OSHA within days of Ronald Reagan's inauguration. Behind this attack were familiar arguments about how the free market could regulate itself and how excessive red tape was a drag on economic growth. But there was a deeper logic here, one that thrives even more strongly today. It is that business is inherently virtuous because hardworking people are getting up every morning to create wealth, not to mention products and services we all use. Businessmen are acting morally by pursuing their self-interest in ways that benefit us all. To expose these upstanding citizens to criminal liability—to put them on the same level as thieves or murderers—is ludicrous. While bad things may happen in business, we are all better off by unfettering those engaged in the virtuous pursuit of self-interest.

There is something to this line of argument. In practice, though, it doesn't much matter whether your son is killed by a parolee who should be behind bars or by an employer who is trying to cut costs. He is still dead. Anyway, business people are not inherently virtuous. They are normal people and are prone to the same temptations as everyone else to put their own self-interest above the safety or well-being of others. If they give into that temptation at the expense of human life, they should be held to account. The problem is not with business generally. Business is good. The problem is with rogue businesses that don't play by the rules.

Today there are fewer people policing workplace safety than there were in 1975, even though the size of the workforce is much bigger. A recent study concluded that it would take OSHA 108 years "to inspect each workplace under its jurisdiction just once." In 2004, the average fine paid for a "serious" violation of safety rules was $872. That's less than many businesses spend on toilet paper every year.[10]

WORKPLACE LAWS aren't the only safeguards that have been eroded, leaving us all more vulnerable. Just look at what happened with Vioxx.

If you're like me, this news story has been a big yawn, with too many layers of complexity to handle over a morning cup of coffee. The facts we have about the case, though, tell a powerful story about personal responsibility in America today.

In 1999, the drug company Merck released Vioxx to treat pain from arthritis. Almost immediately, users of the drug started dying of heart attacks, and the connection to Vioxx seemed clear enough that in 2000 Dr. Sidney Wolfe, a leading industry watchdog, placed the drug on the DO NOT USE list he maintains on his website, www.worstpills.org. He urged the Food and Drug Administration to put a warning label on the drug. The FDA did compel Merck to note a possible link to heart attacks in its labeling, but the drug was allowed to stay on the market. The heart attacks continued. According to some estimates, thousands of people died from health problems caused by Vioxx.[11]

Vioxx was taken off the shelves in September 2004. Not long after that, The Wall Street Journal reported that Merck executives had known about its deadly effects as early as 2000. Two separate clinical trials of the drug allegedly found a correlation between Vioxx and heart attacks. What did Merck do? It tried to explain away and repress the findings, according to inside accounts, even pressuring its own research scientists to change their findings "so that we don't raise concerns." Vioxx, after all, was one of Merck's bestselling drugs, with about $2.5 billion in annual sales. The official line at Merck was that the research was inconclusive.[12]

The allegations against Merck may never be fully proven, but much of the evidence we have suggests this: They knew about the danger. And they didn't do anything. And people died. Thousands of people.

But the story doesn't end there. The Vioxx deaths happened because the government—which is supposed to protect citizens from harm like this, as surely as it protects us from serial killers—wasn't doing its job. The FDA was founded in 1906 to protect Americans from tainted foods and dangerous drugs. It has a budget of only $1.8 billion and a staff of 10,000 to monitor the safety of myriad substances ingested by 300 million Americans. Even this modest effort rankles the right, and abolishing the FDA remains a fond dream of groups like the CATO Institute. In the meantime, a succession of Republican presidents and Congresses has achieved the next best thing—a weakened FDA unable to protect us from behavior that is often intentionally criminal.

Once upon a time the FDA had the resources to run large drug trials when they suspected a drug was dangerous. No longer. The FDA is now geared almost entirely toward the review and approval of new drugs. Once a drug is approved, there is little capacity for evaluating safety problems that become apparent later. The scientists and money just aren't there. And often the will isn't there either. "I would argue that the FDA, as currently configured, is incapable of protecting America from another Vioxx," said

Dr. David Graham, a top reviewer at the agency who had investigated the drug. "We are virtually defenseless."

Graham offered this dire view at a senate hearing in November 2004. A twenty-year veteran at the FDA, he called Vioxx the "single greatest drug safety catastrophe in the history of this country or the history of the world." Graham estimated deaths from Vioxx at 25,000 to 50,000. He compared the toll to two to four commercial airliners crashing every week for five years straight. And all of it could have been prevented, in Graham's view, if the FDA had the resources to get dangerous drugs off the market.[13]

The Vioxx drama isn't over yet, but it is easy to predict how it will go. Merck has already been sued by thousands of Vioxx victims or their surviving relatives and will eventually pay out a huge amount of settlement money. These costs will be passed along to Merck's shareholders, even though they aren't to blame for the disaster. Criminal charges against Merck are unlikely, and if they are made, they will probably be against the company as a whole rather than specific executives.

It may sound bizarre to charge companies with crimes while leaving individuals unmentioned—after all, it is people who make company decisions—but it happens all the time. In 2004, for example, the drug giant Pfizer pleaded guilty to criminal charges involving the drug Neurontin. One of the company's subsidiaries had allegedly promoted the drug in illegal ways that defrauded Medicaid and cost taxpayers millions of dollars. Pfizer agreed to a massive fine, and yet not a single individual in the company admitted wrongdoing or was held criminally responsible for their actions. Numerous other corporate criminal cases in recent years have ended the same way. In fact, it's not uncommon for companies to pay tens of millions of dollars in fines without admitting any wrongdoing at all, much less pleading guilty to any crimes.[14]

We've all heard of victimless crimes, but perpetratorless crimes? Only in America—or, rather, only in corporate America.

CRIME IS DOWN, not out. We have only partly held the line by lowering street crime. Elsewhere we have been losing the fight.

What is needed is a higher and more consistent standard of personal responsibility, so that Americans are safer from *all* forms of predation. On street crime, we can't rest on successes so far. Violent crime remains far above acceptable levels and is deeply corrosive to social trust. Law enforcement needs more resources in order to raise the abysmally low rates of arrest, conviction, and incarceration for violent crimes. It needs more cops in high-crime areas. More prosecutors with more reasonable case loads. More judges. More crime labs. More training in best practices for

all those fighting violent crime. We must keep these resources focused until there are further substantial drops in
murder, rape, assault, domestic abuse, and armed robbery.
Other policies, including mandatory arrest for spousal
abuse, should also be part of a national effort to drastically
reduce violence. We know how to further lower violent
crime, and the *Miranda* ruling and legal aid lawyers are not
what stand in our way.

Nonviolent property crime must also be reduced. Even
when a crime isn't violent, it demands punishment for the
sake of justice and to deter other wrongdoers. The problem is that prosecutors and judges have a very limited menu
of choices. America needs more alternatives to prisons,
which are hugely expensive and often turn minor offenders into more hardened criminals. There are other ways,
such as intensive probationary supervision, to keep nonviolent offenders from again doing wrong. Drug offenses—
as well as other crimes rooted in addiction—should be
dealt with in separate drug courts that compel offenders
to get clean and stay clean, as opposed to sending them to
prison. Community justice solutions are also promising,
compelling offenders to face up to their actions before victims and neighbors. These alternatives are already working in various places on a small scale. They need to be
dramatically scaled up. At the same time, we should invest
far more heavily in effective crime prevention strategies—

particularly community policing which enmeshes police in the neighborhoods they are sworn to protect.

All these steps must be accompanied by a tougher stance on white-collar crime. A justice system can't have moral authority if it mostly focuses on some citizens and some types of crime.

New laws and regulations are not the main answer to cracking down on white-collar crime. There are plenty of those already—too many in some places, to the point that they create a drag on economic growth. We need less red tape around business, not more. Personal responsibility shouldn't have to be at odds with the pursuit of economic freedom. The key is much better enforcement of existing laws that protect the safety, health, and finances of Americans. In a society where high-level defendants can spend $20 million on their criminal defense, as Enron's Kenneth Lay and Jeffrey Skilling did recently, we can't afford to have underpaid, understaffed watchdogs.

OSHA inspectors shouldn't be as common in most workplaces as Elvis. The Securities and Exchange Commission shouldn't fail to vet the majority of quarterly earnings reports of public companies because they don't have enough eyes. The Internal Revenue Service shouldn't give up on the high-hanging fruit of wealthy tax cheats because their investigators are no match for armies of private lawyers. A hobbled FDA shouldn't lack the scientists to independently evaluate drugs or see the pharmaceutical industry as its "client," in David Graham's words. The Justice Department shouldn't reach toothless settlements in major Medicare rip-offs or corporate frauds because it can't sustain a five-year investigation and a nine-month trial. State attorneys general shouldn't ignore "minor" frauds that devastate consumers because they are too busy with the major ones.

The rich and powerful often act as if they are above the law because in many ways they are. We can change that by bolstering the government watchdogs. This is America, not Colombia. If you've done wrong, you shouldn't be able to buy your way out of trouble.

CHAPTER SIX

Honoring Work

O N ELECTION DAY 2004, GEORGE W. BUSH WON West Virginia by 13 percentage points. Bush's sweep of the state—where registered Democrats outnumber Republicans two to one—was impressive. In fact, Bush ran so strong in West Virginia that the Kerry campaign had written the state off well before November.

Exit polls told a familiar story about how Bush won. Voters with only a high school degree went for the president by a 17-point margin. Married voters favored him by 21 points; gun owners by 19 points. Bush performed best in the Appalachian Highland, one of the poorest parts of the state. He even won 41 percent of union members. The issue named most often at the polls was—you guessed it—"moral values"—and Bush won 88 percent of voters who said this was a primary concern.

The values question on the 2004 National Election Pool exit poll has been widely criticized as "poorly devised," preventing "meaningful analysis" of voter concerns, so it is hard to know what was on the minds of West Virginians.[1] A more accurate analysis might well have found that national security was the dominant concern. We do know this: West Virginia is very conservative on social issues. Even many Democrats in the state are pro-life—so pro-life that the two Democratic congressmen from West Virginia each received a "0" rating from NARAL in 2004. Those same Democrats got an "A" from the National Rifle Association. This is a land of traditionalism: hard work in the mines, service to country when the call comes, a commitment to faith and family. The state's culture is deeply populist, making it fertile ground for the tirades of Rush Limbaugh or the homespun speeches of George Bush. The president's line about how the heart and soul of America wasn't in Hollywood went down particularly well here.

West Virginia is easy pickings for conservative culture warriors, and they have been making growing inroads in the state. While West Virginia was one of only six states that Reagan lost in 1980, Bush handily won it in 2000—a victory that secured him the White House.

John Kerry's great hope was that economic woes would neutralize the pull of traditionalism. West Virginia has serious economic problems. The state was largely bypassed by the booming 1990s and has one of the oldest populations in the nation, with nearly one-fifth of households depending upon pension checks and Social Security to make ends meet. Real income has declined for the bottom 20 percent of households since 1979, and West Virginia now has the lowest median income of any state. A quarter of adult West Virginians lack health insurance and one-third make poverty wages.[2]

Despite all this, exit polls showed an odd thing. Yes, most West Virginians thought the economy was in trouble. However, only 28 percent said their family's own economic situation was worse, and as one might predict, these voters went overwhelmingly for Kerry. The remainder of voters said that their situation was either the same or better, and most of these people went for Bush. The economy was bad in West Virginia; it just wasn't bad enough to prove decisive. Even in one of the poorest states, many voters apparently put moral issues or national security concerns above financial worries.

In neighboring Kentucky, also known for its Appalachian poverty, Kerry didn't even have a chance. He again won most of the voters who said their economic situation had worsened, but these voters were outnumbered two to one by people who said things were the same or better. Kentucky's working class lined up solidly behind Bush, including voters making less than $15,000 a year. Moral values, however defined, was the number-one issue by a wide margin. Bush won the state in a landslide.[3]

MASSACHUSETTS LIBERALS weren't always so suspect in these parts. When Democrats think about the lost promise of liberalism, some think back to the Robert F. Kennedy's famous visit to Appalachia in February 1968, a moment when the left appeared to connect with working-class whites. Senator Kennedy traveled two hundred miles through eastern Kentucky, visiting coal-mining towns and one-room schoolhouses and tar-shack homes. Despite his privileged background, RFK had a common touch, mixing compassion with indignation. "Family after family still survives on beans and potatoes or rice, cornbread and fatback," Kennedy said during his visit. "In many of the counties of eastern Kentucky, more than half of the adult men, sometimes over three-quarters, have no work. . . . There have to be people who are going to fight for eastern Kentucky."

This fight wasn't about writing checks, in Kennedy's mind. It was about honoring the hallowed tradition of hard work. "Work is the meaning of what this country is all about," is how Kennedy once put it. "We need it as individuals. We need to sense it in our fellow citizens. And we need it as a society and a people." This same message had been central to Franklin Roosevelt's New Deal, which is one reason why FDR, another patrician by birth, became a deity in parts of Appalachia.[4]

The notion that it was Democrats who honored the virtuous tradition of hard work went unquestioned for decades. Even when the rest of America began drifting right, poor whites in Kentucky kept turning to Democrats for this very reason. A few of the state's Appalachian areas even went for George McGovern during the great Republican landslide of 1972.

Things are different today. In the 2000 election, nine out of ten of Kentucky's poorest counties voted for George W. Bush. He swept poor areas again in 2004. Thanks in part to these voters, the state is now a GOP stronghold, and, by one analysis, has the third most conservative delegation in Congress.[5]

Nothing drives liberals more insane than the belief that blue-collar Americans vote against their own economic interests. How can it be that working stiffs support millionaire Republicans who don't lift a finger on their behalf—and, in fact, are destroying their way of life? How could ordinary people be stupid enough to back politicians who feather the nests of fat cats while gutting things like education or health care? You could understand Joe Six Pack being fooled once or twice by some smooth-talking pol. But this has been going on for decades now.

Or has it? The political scientist Larry Bartels has shown that lower-income whites haven't actually become more Republican or more likely to vote based on social issues like abortion. Another political scientist, Jeffrey

Stonecash, makes a similar case in his book *Class and Party in American Politics*. Both observe that the defection of working-class whites from the Democrats has been mostly confined to the South. Nationally, voting behavior now tracks more closely along income than in the past. Poorer voters more consistently vote Democratic; wealthier voters more regularly go for Republicans. Also, contrary to myth, poorer white voters do tend to see big differences between the political parties on economic issues, as well as on other matters.[6]

Clearly the battle for the white working class isn't over yet; not by a long shot. On the other hand, poorer whites have never been a lock for the Democrats. In the eight presidential elections since 1972, only half of low-income whites voted Democratic on average. The other half were pivotal to GOP dominance.[7]

To win these voters, centrist Democrats have long argued that the party should tack to the middle on cultural issues, as Clinton tried to do. Others, such as author Thomas Frank, say that Democrats have lost the heartland because they abandoned economic populism. If liberals could revive that spirit—if they stopped flying Gulfstreams and driving Land Rovers, if they stood up for welders instead of whales, if they blew off Wall Street and got down with Main Street—poorer whites would come around.

This comeback plan has gained quite a bit of ground in liberal circles over recent years. It informed Gore's 2000 run, in which the former centrist vice president reinvented himself as a fire-breathing populist. "We're for the people, they're for the powerful!" Gore chanted. It was reflected in John Edwards's bid for the presidency, in which the one-time millionaire trial lawyer invoked a vision of "two Americas." And it is the solution offered by *What's the Matter With Kansas?*, one of the most-read progressive tracts of recent times. If the liberal base of the Democratic Party has a clear vision of how to win power, economic populism is it.

It's easy to see the appeal of this vision. The crunch on low- and middle-income Americans is severe: unaffordable health insurance, stagnant wages, sky-high housing prices, inadequate child care. How long can Americans tolerate this abuse? Not much longer, I would think. In an age of insecurity, Democrats should be able to regain dominance by learning again to push the old economic buttons.

And maybe they can. But there are two problems here that liberals need to reckon with. One is that it can be perfectly rational to elevate values above economic concerns, even if you are not among the swells. If you're pro-life, you might well think that trying to stop over a million abortions a year is more important than getting a raise. If you're a parent, it might be reasonable to be more afraid of your teenage daughter getting pregnant or hooked on meth than losing your health coverage. If you're married, you could worry more about your spouse having an affair than your boss sacking you. Moral concerns like this are not nothing. Also, liberals vote their values all the time. No one asks, "What's the matter with Cambridge?"

The second problem is that in places like Kentucky and West Virginia, many liberal economic policies aren't much easier to sell than the theory of evolution. Democratic schemes to help the little guy often fall flat . . . with the little guy.

Now why is that?

I got one answer to this question when I traveled to Kentucky and met with Kent Ostrander, a leading conservative activist in the state. As Ostrander—an evangelical Christian—explained it, family values and economic conservatism go together naturally. Most social and economic challenges, he said, boil down "to the individual's duty to regulate himself." Liberals like to blame the system for everything, Ostrander said, while conservatives assume that individuals can make choices and act on those choices. This is true whether it comes to keeping a marriage intact or keeping food on the table. "If the individual cannot govern himself, than certainly the government is not going to be able to do it," Ostrander said.

A great many religious conservatives like Ostrander preach economic self-reliance, although scholars debate whether this holds as a general rule. The sociologist Stephen Hart has insisted that "religious traditionalism does *not* lead to economic conservatism," while another so-ciologist, Wayne Baker—echoing Max Weber—finds that if you're a traditionalist when it comes to family and reli-gion, you're probably also a fan of the free market.[8]

The truth may lie somewhere in between. The deeply traditionalist Catholic Church has issued strident calls for economic justice. Right-wing evangelicals, on the other hand, almost always back the GOP's fiscal conservatism. One possible reason that many evangelicals take such a tough stance on work and self-reliance is that their faith is very individualistic. Unlike Catholicism with its strict hierarchy, or mainline Protestantism, which can be very community oriented, evangelical Christianity stresses the personal dimensions of faith. If it's up to the individual to connect with Jesus Christ and find salvation, it's a small step to demanding that the individual also take full re-sponsibility for their economic well-being.[9]

Another view of why social and economic conservatism might go hand-in-hand comes from the linguist George Lakoff, who blasted out of obscurity not long ago to be-come a guru to Democratic leaders such as Nancy Pelosi. In Lakoff's view, most conservatives subscribe to the "strict father model," which holds that we all need to learn self-discipline in order to be good and moral people—which means, among other things, delaying sexual gratification and honoring family commitments. A strict father teaches discipline to children by setting rules and meting out punishment. But the free market is another great disciplinarian, since everyone has to work hard to survive and work requires that you be responsible and diligent. Work means putting aside short-term desires, like the urge to sleep late or smoke a joint at lunch. The smaller the social safety net, the harder you'll work to keep your balance, exercising the self-discipline that leads to better behavior in other parts of life, such as marriage and family.[10]

Thus the squared circle: Cutting social programs *helps* working families. Even someone who isn't doing so well might subscribe to this logic.

The false consciousness argument made by Thomas Frank offers another take on what's going on, and it's a thesis that has been advanced by others as well. A few decades ago, a scholar named John Gaventa argued that the working class of Appalachia didn't challenge an economic system that oppressed them because they couldn't see that there *was* a system. They saw the economy as a natural phenomenon, not as a manmade set of arrangements that benefited some people at the expense of others. Gaventa called this hidden power structure the "third face of power." People could be oppressed and not even know it. They might even help their oppressors.[11]

These days, in an era of globalization, it is particularly easy to think that no one is in control. Again and again we're told that lost jobs and benefits, as well as rising inequality, stem from a changing economy and that there isn't much we can do about this. When John Kerry ran for president he dwelled on a few small ideas about helping working-class Americans, such as penalizing corporations that outsourced jobs. Yet even he didn't seem to believe these steps would have much effect.

"The economic issues are complicated and are often beyond people," comments Kent Ostrander. "The social issues are black and white. They're simple, especially if you're religious." Ostrander added another explanation for why people might vote on social issues: "A lot of the poorer people around here are content," he said. "They have a little house they've lived in for a long time. They see their friends, their family. They're happy."

In many counties in Kentucky, more than half of families have incomes below $15,000 a year and live in deteriorating trailers or shacks. A quarter of all workers in the state make poverty-level wages; one in five lack health insurance. It's hard to imagine anyone would be content with such conditions. On the other hand, Ostrander may be on to something. Kentucky is far more prosperous today than when Bobby Kennedy visited the state. Back then, a great many homes in Appalachia lacked indoor plumbing and one-third of all residents lived in poverty. Hunger was common.

Now nearly everyone has plumbing—and often satellite TV, too—and the region's poverty rate is not far above the national average. Even the poorest Kentuckians have a standard of living that would have put them in the middle class forty years ago. Recent times in particular have been good for Kentucky. The poorest fifth of Kentucky families saw income gains of 23 percent during the 1990s, a much better improvement than in many states. Kentucky ranks high in housing affordability and low in taxes and energy costs.[12]

Add these facts to the traditionalist view about self-reliance and the ways that economic issues seem to be off the table, and the voting patterns of working-class Kentuckians start to make more sense. GOP policies may be outrageously unfair—one analysis found that the wealthiest 1 percent of Kentuckians received $33,194 on average from Bush's tax cuts, while the bottom 20 percent got about $51—but the bigger story for poor whites in Kentucky has been a rise in living standards since the 1960s. Compared to the past, the glass might well seem half full to many poorer voters. Kentucky's poor whites simply don't worry about basic survival the way they once did.[13]

Even if things were tougher in Kentucky, it's not clear how far liberals would get here with their typical approaches. Democrats are good at appealing to the economic *interests* of lower-income whites, but less effective at appealing to their economic *values*. In some cases, liberal arguments seem more suitable to Western European voters than to the many Americans who embrace a vision of economic freedom that hinges on self-reliance and individual effort.

The political scientist Jennifer Hochschild once commented that blind faith in the American Dream is unfounded, since plenty of people who work hard never succeed, but "it's all we have" and, like it or not, it will always be the dominant way we think about opportunity. Others have gone farther, arguing that the American Dream is the glue that holds America together in the absence of a common ethnic or national heritage. When a country is founded upon an idea, it's kind of hard to question that idea.

If that is true, and I think it is, it explains much. Liberals have a bad habit of contesting the premise of America. They say: No, opportunity doesn't exist for all, and no, hard work won't set you free. They offer a mountain of evidence to back up this view and assume these arguments will ring true given people's own life experiences. Instead, many Americans hear something else. They hear liberals trying to dash their hopes. Or they hear liberals talking down to them, pitying them for their difficulties and telling them they're in such bad shape that someone else needs to bail them out.

Republicans have seized on this mistake. They don't yet own the American Dream, but they've made a pretty good down payment on it in recent decades—whether through the "morning again" appeals of Ronald Reagan or the "ownership society" of George W. Bush. Republicans not only tell people they can take charge of their own destiny and be, in Bush's words, "truly free"; they have also typecast liberals as the enemy of such freedom, what with all their big-government schemes for taxes, red tape, zoning rules, class-action suits, hiring quotas, and so on. Liberals are for a Swedish nanny state, we're told, and have presided over the "death of common sense." Conservatives, on the other hand, embrace the frontier spirit.

Liberals haven't always been trapped in this corner. At various times their vision for economic freedom has trumped a narrower, laissez-faire notion of liberty. Liberals once championed the ideals of individual effort and responsibility—while also promising to tame market forces that fostered insecurity and a tyranny of the haves. Earlier liberals promised to make us free by giving each of us the ability to achieve our full potential. They blended themes of self-reliance with a moral insistence that America was a community and that we had to look out for one another.

Can this lost formula be rediscovered? I don't see why not.

IT ALL STARTS with work. Work is among the most cherished of traditional values. Quite apart from its link to religious faith, hard work has been a central pillar of the American experiment, which rejected feudalism in favor of the belief that people could shape their own destiny. In the Old World, no amount of work could transform your place in society, which was determined at birth. Class standing derived from land ownership, and Europe's land, owned by royalty and dynastic families, seldom changed hands. Once a commoner, always a commoner. Work was about survival and service to others. Self-invention was an unknown concept.

Work had a different meaning in the New World. Land was plentiful and could become the basis of wealth for those who put in the effort. Free white men of any class could move upward with sweat and toil, going as far as their willpower would take them. This notion that hard work could secure personal freedom was radical and dazzling, and it has retained its hold on our imagination—so much so that whichever political party best champions the idea has a good shot at dominating politics.

Conservatives owned work at the height of the Robber Baron era in the late nineteenth century. They promised, against all evidence, that anyone who worked hard would succeed in the new industrial economy. Just look at how Andrew Carnegie rose from rags to riches, they said. Read your Horatio Alger. If you didn't work hard enough or smart enough, it wasn't the fault of the system; it meant you lacked virtue and deserved to fall by the wayside. Social Darwinism justified a society in which there was no regulation of wages and scant provision for the unemployed or disabled.

A century ago, progressive reformers began to wrestle work away from conservatives. The great labor leader Eugene V. Debs used the patriotic language of "liberty" to blast the industrial overclass for enslaving the American everyman and subverting the promise of a fair return for one's efforts. Theodore Roosevelt, and later William Howard Taft, depicted corporate trusts as conspiracies that stacked the deck against small businessmen and doomed even the hardest-working entrepreneurs to failure.

Franklin Roosevelt was masterful at laying claim to the ideals of self-creation and personal liberty through hard work. In his 1936 speech to the Democratic Convention, Roosevelt decried industrial barons who had imposed a "new despotism," and said that "the average man once more confronts the problem that faced the Minute Man." He exhorted America to fight a "new industrial dictatorship" that crushed "individual initiative." FDR than spelled out his vision of freedom: "Liberty requires opportunity to make a living—a living decent according to the standard of the time, a living which gives man not only enough to live by, but something to live for. . . . Today we stand committed to the proposition that freedom is no half-and-half affair. If the average citizen is guaranteed equal opportunity in the polling place, he must have equal opportunity in the market place."

This theme would frame the liberal message about work for another three decades. It was the message that Robert F. Kennedy would take into Appalachia and to other impoverished areas of America. Had Kennedy become president, rewarding the virtue of work might well have been central to his economic policies. But Kennedy was dead five months after his trip to Kentucky, and liberal control of the moral high ground of work didn't last beyond the 1960s. Conservatives seized this high ground as welfare rolls expanded. Liberals came to be seen as antiwork—as coddlers who believed in "something for nothing."

The rest of this history is well known. Republicans bludgeoned Democrats with the welfare issue for a generation. Distorted media images of welfare played into claims that everyone on the dole was black and undeserving. The actual facts about welfare—that it was mostly used by whites, for short periods of time, and for good reasons—didn't matter.[14] The very idea of welfare ticked off many Americans, and the system spawned enough actual dependency and bad behavior to create the political equivalent of a nuclear weapon. Conservatives rose to power not just by connecting to the white working class on social issues and national security, but also by defending one of the traditional values most prized by these voters—that of hard work.

The tragedy in all this is that welfare distracted attention from the *real* betrayal of work. Welfare moved to center stage just as the industrial era came to a close, ending an entire way of life—one in which a person with little education could achieve the American Dream through disciplined toil alone. In a farce of politics, much more moral indignation would be vented at a system that gave chump change to a few million needy families than at the wholesale humbling of blue-collar America by a new logic of corporate self-interest. Welfare queens in Cadillacs would generate more outrage than the rise of a postindustrial order that devalued manual labor, destroyed unions, left whole manufacturing regions to rust, and lowered wages. Workers were encouraged to complain more about the run-down subsidized apartments of single mothers than about the third or fourth mansions bought by CEOs as their pay soared from forty times what the average worker made in 1980 to three hundred times by the 1990s.

It's too bad George Orwell didn't live to see this one.

Most Americans have only the foggiest sense of where their electricity comes from, and few would ever guess that half the nation's electricity is generated by coal. In today's information age, it is hard to remember that coal miners even exist, and yet without them the lights would go out pretty fast. American power plants burn three times as much coal today as in 1970—a billion tons a year. This is criminal given global warming, but that's not the miners'

fault. Next time you flick on a light switch, think of someone working in the darkness, five days a week. And say a
word of thanks.

Coal mining is unlike other jobs. It involves descend-
ing deep underground—sometimes one thousand feet or
more—and working in dangerous conditions. While coal
mining is a lot safer than it used to be, plenty of miners still
die every year. Sometimes they die by the dozen, as happened in West Virginia in December 2005, in an accident
later linked to the lax enforcement of mine safety rules.
Miners are killed by toxic gases or from explosions or cave-
ins. Many more are badly injured. The real risks, though,
kick in during retirement: about 1,500 coal miners die annually from black lung disease.

The mining regions of Appalachia have always been
home to Americans less educated and more conservative
than average. But it was in these places, along with the mill
towns that produced steel and other sites of manufacturing, where twentieth-century liberals forged a synthesis
between the traditional value of hard work and the collectivist notion that we must band together to make capitalism be "good." Coal mining lent itself to this synthesis.
Miners worked in groups, crowding into the elevator that
took them down into the mines every morning and up
again at quitting time. They looked out for each other underground and above ground, too, living close together in

the same communities. Everyone was in this job together. And yet there was no better test of a man's individual mettle than his ability to wield a pickax or sledgehammer for hours on end, battering off large hunks of coal and heaving them into a rail car.

Mining has changed a lot in recent decades. Though America uses more coal than ever, good jobs in mining have been fast disappearing. Twenty-six thousand jobs have been lost in coal mining in the past decade alone, with devastating effects.[15] These jobs are not being shipped to China; they are being eliminated by new technologies and mining techniques. Heavy machines have replaced teams of workers, and more coal comes from surface mines. One common technique is to blast off the top of entire mountains to get at the coal.

Many mining jobs that do remain are nonunion, with lower pay and fewer benefits. The United Mine Workers has been fighting union busting for decades, and sometimes winning. But it is not clear that anything can or should be done about job losses in coal mining. If far fewer people must work in pitch blackness, breathing in coal dust, to keep America's power grid on, that seems like a good thing to me.

The problem is that other well-paying jobs aren't coming along to replace the lost mining jobs. The median hourly wage in West Virginia is about twelve dollars an hour. A job at Wal-Mart—the state's largest employer—

pays less than that. If you have a college degree, you're in better shape; unfortunately, nearly half of all high school graduates in West Virginia never get such a degree and the state ranks almost last nationwide in college affordability. The loss of coal jobs has taken away a path to security that led from high school to full-time work with benefits, to home ownership, and finally to a dignified retirement.[16]

This same thing is happening in one manufacturing sector after another, a trend that seems to be accelerating with the faltering of General Motors. Other secure jobs are disappearing, too, with the airlines laying off tens of thousands of workers and former lifelong employers like IBM regularly downsizing. Many of the new jobs being created pay terribly. About 30 million Americans—a fifth of the labor force—make less than $8.50 an hour.[17]

WE KNOW ALL THIS. We have known it for a long time. So why haven't Democrats parlayed these facts into a new moral story about the betrayal of work—one that could firmly supplant the thirty-year conservative rant about welfare?

Perhaps it's the elitism of party leaders, as many suggest. Maybe the problem with a guy like John Kerry is that he spent so much time shuttling between his mansions in Sun Valley, Martha's Vineyard, Beacon Hill, and Georgetown—did I get them all?—that when it came time to talk the old Democratic talk, he didn't know the words. Maybe if the Democrats stopped nominating kite boarders who "look French" they'd get someplace. Or maybe they'd rediscover economic populism if they stopped taking big checks from corporate America, as Robert Kuttner suggested long ago in his Democratic obituary, *The Life of the Party.*

Before he was locked in a closet by the Kerry campaign, John Edwards got traction among moderate audiences with his speeches about "two Americas." He reminded us that when Democrats tell a values-based story about the betrayal of work and the fall of working-class America, people listen—at least up to a point. Things can get dicey when the talk turns to solutions.

In arguing that welfare betrayed work, conservatives offered a simple solution: Get rid of handouts and make people responsible for themselves. That solution fit naturally with American individualism and the belief that opportunity is available for all.

Democrats face a harder sales job. Most liberal solutions to the betrayal of work boil down to some form of collective action, whether it's getting more people organized in labor unions or using government to raise the minimum wage and expand the safety net. The problem, though, is that collective thinking—the notion that we are all in it together—comes much less naturally to Americans nowadays. Institutions like government that once embodied common hopes are now distrusted, and not just because we loathe the Department of Motor Vehicles. Given the choice, many people would rather do their own thing than compromise their autonomy to work with others.

Meanwhile, the workplace has also turned more individualistic and atomized. Far fewer people work in coal mines and steel mills and big auto plants—places where it was easy to understand one's common interest with others, and where a fusion between the ideals of hard work and shared struggle was easy to grasp. Workers are more alone now, both physically and psychologically. The same trends that have undermined the value of work have also isolated people in their own predicaments—as temporary employees or independent contractors or some other fleeting figure in our seven-jobs-over-a-lifetime economy. Unions are virtually defunct in the private sector, not just because of union busting, which has gotten worse, but because it's harder to organize a fragmented labor force.

The more alone we are, the more alone we feel. When the screws are turned on people, their reflex these days is to pull inward and individualize their problems. The losers in America have always been told to blame themselves, not the system, but now they do so more than ever, encouraged by claims that a character defect lies behind every story of economic hardship. The solution to our woes, we are taught, is to focus ever more intently on our self-interest: Try harder, get up earlier, make smarter investments, take bigger risks—and oppose taxes or social programs that cut into our paychecks. The potential for a reinforcing dynamic is obvious. As widening insecurity fans an every-man-for-himself mood, it undermines common efforts to make things better, which leads to even greater insecurity and further insularity.

It doesn't help that the media cover the wealthy around the clock, with endless stories of the self-made rich that blot out far less sexy statistics about downward mobility. People may know intellectually that the traditional virtue of hard work doesn't count as much as it used to, and they may know that the deck is stacked more solidly against them. Yet it is easy in the age of Powerball and the Google Guys for them to imagine that they will be the one who defies the odds.

THESE DYNAMICS aren't insurmountable. I got some ideas about how to work around them in a conversation with a SuperShuttle driver in Dallas named Steve Hicks.

SuperShuttles are those blue vans that work the airports and hotels in many cities. The company calls itself a "shared ride provider." I met Steve late one night while traveling and we started having a friendly conversation about the ways of the SuperShuttle. Gas prices had recently spiked, following Hurricane Katrina, and Steve was hurting. He was making $700 or $800 less per month because of higher prices at the pump. The last time he'd gotten crunched like this was when the health insurance premium for him and his wife hit $1,200 a month. He dropped the coverage. Not buying gas, though, was out of the question.

Why such troubles for an airport shuttle driver? Well, it turned out that Steve was no mere employee; he was an "owner-operator," which meant that he had bought the blue van from SuperShuttle and pays all the costs of operating it. SuperShuttle doesn't pay Steve a dime. On the contrary, he pays the company a set fee every month, as well as a percentage of his earnings, for access to passengers. The money can be good, especially if he works very long days, but things were getting tight. "There's a lot of people just scraping by," he said of himself and others.

SuperShuttle drivers didn't always shoulder so much risk. The company, which was founded in 1983, operated for two decades on the traditional employee model. It moved to a franchise approach a few years ago. Under the new structure, "the driver is in business for himself," a top SuperShuttle executive said, in announcing the move in 2002. "This eliminates some variable costs that are very hard for us to control and allows us to keep quality standards in place."[18] Unfortunately, the new capitalists minted by SuperShuttle are no better than the company at controlling "variable costs," as Steve Hicks found out, but these individuals are less able to weather such ups and downs.

Steve didn't blame anyone for his problems. The only way he saw to do better was to work more hours, which is why he was out late on a weeknight, when most people would rather be at home with their families. Steve is book-ing every pickup he can handle, and then some.

I asked Steve whether he thought elected leaders could help him, perhaps with cheaper health care.

Steve said he didn't know much about politics. The economy was the biggest issue for Steve, but "to tell you the truth," he said, "I don't really know much about the differ-ence between the two parties—except that the Democrats want to give handouts to people who don't work and the Republicans are for helping you make something of your-self through business."

"Wait a minute," I said. "Didn't Bill Clinton try to help everyone get health insurance?"

"Both sides talk about health care every election, but they never do anything about it," Steve said. He's given up on that one. If a politician were serious about this issue, Steve might listen.

Many people are working as Steve does: for them-selves. More than ten million Americans are now self-employed or are contract workers, and their numbers are likely to grow, driven by cost-cutting companies, new technologies that make outsourcing easier, and the desire among many people to gain more control of their time. So, too, will the trend in large firms toward shorter job tenures and diminished job security. Like it or not, the reinvention of America as a "free agent nation" may only be getting started.

While unions may yet experience a renewal—witness the exciting victories in organizing janitors in Texas and home-health aides in Los Angeles—it is hard to see anything on the horizon that will recreate the solidarity of yesterday's shop floor. Honoring the value of work now means something more than just a better deal for workers who punch a clock every morning. It means supporting those people who dream of more freedom and autonomy even as we build stronger forms of community that bind us to one another and offer protection from misfortune.

America must make the SuperShuttle model succeed. There are plenty of people like Steven Hicks who would rather be an "owner-operator" than an employee, and that's not a bad thing. Small businesses create three-quarters of all new jobs, and are more likely to put profits back into their communities. Also, one reason SuperShuttle moved to a franchise approach is that it had tremendous turnover among its drivers, which meant poorer service for customers and lots of training costs for the company. Better pay and benefits might have helped retain some employees, but driving an airport shuttle is the kind of job that people tend to hold on their way to something else.

The "owner-operators," though, stick with the job, and you can see why. Steve Hicks actually has a shot at building a lucrative career. When he's not driving his Super-Shuttle, he can hire somebody else to drive it for him. If he makes good enough money, he can buy another van—or two or three vans. Maybe one day he won't have to drive at all.

At the same time, all of Steve's dreams could vanish in a single disaster: a period without work because a terrorist incident closes the airports. An illness that leads to personal bankruptcy. A spike in oil prices. More people want the freedom that comes with being their own boss, but lately it's gotten harder to be Steve Hicks, not easier.

We can change that.

CONSERVATIVES CONNECT DEEPLY with Americans when they talk about empowering individuals to get rich—and liberals connect equally deeply when they demand basic levels of security for all. So why not a new vision of economic life that offers both at the same time? First and foremost, this means sustaining high levels of growth. Whether you want more millionaires or more people climbing out of poverty, nothing beats boom times. We caught a brief glimpse of that during the late 1990s when everyone who worked hard reaped rewards; wages rose for those at the bottom even as the ranks of the rich exploded. The path to more prosperity like this is through much greater investments in education, infrastructure, and the technologies of the future. A Manhattan Project for alternative energy would be one way to help build tomorrow's economy. Creating universal access to wireless broadband would be another. Fiscal sanity in Washington is also essential—enough borrowing, already—as is re-forming a tax code that favors the inherited rich over those who work for a living while doling out perks to yes-terday's industries.

Second, we need to update our expectations of busi-ness. If Steve Hicks can't afford health care for himself, he's certainly not going to provide it for some driver he hires. If you're in business, you should be able to focus on making money. You shouldn't have to deal with the astronomical cost of health benefits or the piles of paperwork that sur-round pension programs or unemployment insurance. The amount of time and money that goes into dealing with employee benefits is ludicrous. It's especially devastat-ing for small businesses. Ditto for the broader sea of red tape that current or would-be business owners must fight every day, like mindless licensing requirements or archaic fire safety regulations. As David Osborne and other advo-cates of "reinventing government" have argued, there are better ways to regulate business and protect the common good. Fewer burdens on business will make it easier for people to pursue personal freedom through entrepreneur-ial risk-taking. It will also mean more prosperity overall.

The smartest thing we could do along these lines is modernize and expand America's commitment to social insurance. Whether you can survive an illness without going bankrupt or endure a long stint of unemployment or retire comfortably shouldn't depend on whom you happen to work for. Basic protections should be universal and follow us wherever we go. Everyone should enjoy a minimum level of security—health care, a pension, unemployment insurance, workers' compensation—whether they work for IBM or as a SuperShuttle owner-operator. Real freedom requires strong community. If we have each other's backs, all of us can dream bigger and take more risks in the quest to take charge of our destiny. The golden age of employer-provided benefits was nice while it lasted, but it's collapsing fast. The linking of work and social benefits is an anachronism of a faded industrial era, not the way of the future in a global economy where U.S. businesses need every edge they can get. So let's get on with creating universal protections—for example, by expanding Medicare into a national health system that covers everyone and by creating portable 401(k)-type retirement accounts for all Americans.

Third, we should retain welfare rules that demand work from everyone. Those who get up every morning shouldn't subsidize those who sleep in. Anyone who can work should work. But if you work, you deserve to be rewarded with a wage that covers basic living expenses in your area. Nothing devalues work more than subpoverty wages, especially at a time when some people get paid so much for so little effort. We can't do much about a management guru getting $40,000 for spending half a day at a corporate retreat (except tax that money at a higher rate), but we can better reward the efforts of those at the bottom. There are two ways to do this: by raising the minimum wage far above where it now is, or by subsidizing wages with tax credits. A combination makes the most sense. Jacking up the minimum wage somewhat will be no big deal for most businesses. Many states have raised their minimums without adverse effects, and the federal minimum could rise substantially. But Steve Hicks won't be able to expand his business if he has to pay his drivers $11 an hour. Thus a higher minimum wage should work in concert with a greatly expanded Earned Income Tax Credit that covers all low-wage workers. Credits should be pegged to the cost of living in your area and the size of your household. If you and your husband live in Little Rock and have a combined income of $24,000 but need $32,000 to meet basic expenses, the subsidy would be $8,000. If you make $24,000 and live on Long Island, you'd get a much bigger subsidy. This program will cost a bundle. But as far as I know, there is no other way to ensure the value of work in a low-wage, high-cost society. If you have a better idea, I'm in the phone book.

Fourth, let's renew the promise of affordable college for any qualified student who wants it. Higher education has long spelled more freedom in America, even as it demanded self-discipline and sacrifice. Once, just about anyone could afford tuition at a state university system that embodied the ideal of meritocracy. Now such tuition is out of reach of many families and financial aid is evaporating. Stupid rich kids go to college at a higher rate than smart poor kids. That won't do, not in America. In her book *Strapped*, Tamara Draut has spelled out a "Contract for College" that would use a combination of grants and loans to ensure that every qualified high school student could afford to attend a public university. Enabling such self-improvement won't solve the problem of too few decent jobs to go around in America. It will ensure fairer competition for those jobs.[19]

Fifth, let's create a real ownership society. Private property is the ultimate route to freedom. If you work hard enough to own a home or business, you'll enjoy more choices and more security. A great many Americans aspire to reach this goal and we should help them get there. Privatizing Social Security and creating more tax shelters for the rich, as President Bush has proposed, isn't the way. As it stands, the lion's share of the mortgage interest deduction, as well as tax subsidies for retirement savings, already go to people who don't need help. It's time to refocus asset-building efforts on those people who haven't risen to the middle class—the people who badly need a hand with a down payment on a house or a small business loan, or even with starting a savings account. We should start early, with Children's Savings Accounts—or "Baby Bonds," as they are called in Britain. These accounts would provide a nest egg for newborns and match their deposits over the years. Likewise, Individual Development Accounts for adults, which already exist on a small scale, should be scaled up. Tax deductions for mortgage interest and retirement savings should be restructured to primarily benefit lower- and middle-income working families. Community economic development models that promote local entrepreneurship should be expanded. The great thing about assets is that they are not just a path toward freedom; research shows that they also foster a greater sense of responsibility. As the old saying goes, no one has ever washed a rented car.[20]

Expensive policies to create more opportunity have often been a tough sell in America, and that won't soon change. At this point, with the federal coffers dry, more money for such efforts must come from the concentrated wealth at the very top of our society, which will take a big fight. Yet the basic idea is hard to refute: *America must be a community where everyone can achieve personal freedom and basic security through hard work.*

CHAPTER SEVEN

Who Cares About the Poor?

I N DECEMBER 2005, AS THE HOLIDAY SEASON BEGAN, Congress finished work on another federal budget. Thanks to years of Mastercard fiscal policy, the deficit raged out of control, and this year—with conservatives howling about bloated government—the Republican leadership pledged to finally get serious about cutting spending.

Aid to the poor would not have seemed an obvious place to save money. After all, 2005 was the year of Hurricane Katrina—a disaster that pulled back the curtain on hardcore poverty, triggering a rare bout of concern about the less fortunate. Even in December, three months after Katrina, thousands of evacuees still lived in tents. Low-income Americans had taken an additional hit after the hurricane when fuel prices soared. Now, as the cold

weather kicked in, many families were forced to choose between heat and food. If the poor deserved anything as
2005 came to a close, it was a great big Christmas present.

That isn't what they got. Instead, Congress went after
antipoverty programs with a chain saw. They slashed
spending for Medicaid, which provides health care to the
neediest, and passed new rules to make it harder for
people to get on Medicaid in the first place. They gutted
a successful initiative that helps low-income women col-
lect child support from absent fathers, and they whacked
funds from foster-care programs that enable abandoned
children to be raised by their grandparents rather than
by strangers. They delayed payments to poor people with
disabilities and reduced aid to needy college students.
They also increased the work requirements for parents
on welfare—while underfunding child care by billions of
dollars.[1]

Oh, and one other detail about this budget: It cut taxes
for the very wealthiest Americans and actually increased
the deficit.

More than a hundred religious leaders and advocates
for the poor were arrested in a protest on Capitol Hill as
the budget cutters finished their work. They kneeled and
prayed for a "moral budget" before being led away. News-
papers like the *New York Times* ran outraged editorials. Social justice listserves went into overdrive. But nobody else
seemed to notice.

At one level, the Christmas budget cuts tell a simple story about the dark side of democracy: Legislators hammer the poor because they can. People at the bottom of the income ladder make up an impotent part of the electorate. Even if low-income citizens voted more, or always voted their economic interests, they would be easy prey in a nation that is predominantly middle class. A few years back, the pollster Mark Mellman held extensive interviews with state legislators and policy makers nationwide, asking them about issues of child poverty. Most of the leaders said that the plight of poorer Americans wasn't on their radar. Mellman concluded, "Alleviating poverty is not a top priority for legislators, in part because they believe their states face difficult budget straits and because most do not believe their constituents truly care about the issue."[2] Lawmakers from poor districts often worry about poverty, but they are outnumbered. So when it comes time to divvy up the budget pie, the poor get only crumbs.

In past times, many cold-hearted legislators faced punishment at the polls as better-off Americans rose to defend the less fortunate. Now it appears that narrow self-interest is more likely to carry the day. A majority may not support the GOP's harsh policies, but neither do they much object when their leaders kick those who are already down. Many middle-class voters, for example, are far more concerned about getting rid of the Alternative Minimum Tax than with protecting Medicaid. Wealthier Americans, in turn, seem perfectly content to pocket gains from the huge tax cuts enacted since 2001—even if doing so leads to fiscal triage of the ugliest sort.

In Washington, as well as in many state capitals, the notion that we have a responsibility toward the most vulnerable among us is fast becoming a quaint anachronism. Year after year lawmakers are putting the squeeze on aid to the neediest, moving us closer toward a society in which the weak fall by the wayside. The Social Darwinism of the Gilded Age has returned in modern form, and by the looks of things, the worst is yet to come.

The triumph of self-interest is not surprising. So much of what we see and hear encourages us to look out for ourselves. For thirty years we've heard that the more we all focus on our own economic interests, the better everyone will do. We've also been told that government can't do anything right, especially when it comes to helping the poor. And while America has plenty of selfless heroes battling social ills, few people have ever heard of them. Instead, our leading role models are those who have piled up the most money and status. Brad and Angelina may go to an African orphanage now and again, but mainly they are busy being rich and famous. The spirit of our age directs our attention enviously upward, to what we could have, as opposed to downward in concern for others. We don't see the homeless people we step over, but do notice the opulent townhouses along the same street. We're more likely to feel aggrieved at not being able to afford nicer restaurants than to feel fortunate that we get hot meals at all.

Such are the perils of mass affluence, you might say. But at other times affluence has worked the other way, giving people the leeway to think beyond their own self-interest. What's notable about recent decades is how much permission we feel to turn inward, no matter how much our fellow citizens need help. Data from the General Social Survey indicates that empathy for the vulnerable remains the norm—90 percent of Americans said that people should be willing to help the needy—but it doesn't translate into the political realm.[3]

The story doesn't end there. What's unique about the new Social Darwinism is that those in charge don't consciously subscribe to Herbert Spencer's ideas about "survival of the fittest." Many see themselves as good people who are helping the poor, and behind the budget cuts is a clear moral vision about how to combat poverty. The vision is embraced by GOP leaders and the conservative intelligentsia. It is preached from megachurch pulpits and practiced by faith-based initiatives in the inner city. You hear it from Bill O'Reilly—or from your uncle at a family barbecue. Two decades ago this thinking was inchoate. Now it is moving toward dominance.

Understanding the vision isn't easy, since it is not exactly intuitive. But the vision isn't going away. And if you are interested in its moral logic, the best place to start is with the ideas of Marvin Olasky.

Olasky wouldn't be recognized on the street by ten out of ten Americans, but he may be the single most influential poverty expert of the last twenty years. He is the kind of intellectual action figure who leaps forth every so often into politics: the mild-mannered academic who publishes the right book at the right time, buys a few new suits, and is catapulted to stardom. Before 1992 Olasky was just another hardworking professor at a regional university—in this case, teaching journalism at the University of Texas at Austin. He churned out books and articles on such topics as how the media covered abortion or on the history of corporate public relations. In the 1980s, however, he became interested in poverty, influenced by Robert Woodson, an African American leader who rejected big-government solutions in favor of small-neighborhood efforts. Olasky also participated in a working group on Third World poverty that concluded that this problem was spiritual as much as material: Most poor people simply didn't think they could ever change their situation. Money by itself wouldn't lift them up; their attitudes had to change, too.

This viewpoint resonated with Olasky. While Olasky had been raised in a Jewish family in Boston and was an atheist and a Marxist in high school—as well as a member of the Communist Party—he became a born-again Christian in 1976. He came to believe deeply in self-discipline and strict biblical morality. As Olasky understood history, it used to be common for antipoverty efforts to focus on personal responsibility—as opposed to liberalism's emphasis on the structures that cause poverty. He decided that someone needed to unearth this forgotten history. Olasky plunged into a book project that looked at charity efforts going back to Colonial times.

The book was *The Tragedy of American Compassion.* It argued that well before big government came along, thousands of local charities had provided help to the needy—help that was more effective than bureaucratic social programs because charities became deeply involved with the poor and pushed them to change their lives. The most effective of these efforts were guided by religion, Olasky said. Earlier wars on poverty had been waged with a combination of "loving compassion and rigorous discipline." In particular, most charities followed Apostle Paul's edict that "If a man will not work, he shall not eat." America went astray, Olasky said, when it adopted a something-for-nothing approach to charity.[4]

Olasky wrote most of his book as a visiting fellow at the Heritage Foundation, then struggled to find a home for it. The small conservative publishing house Regnery picked it up in 1992 but didn't put much into its marketing, and the book sank without a trace. Then, in 1993, Olasky received an invitation to meet with George W. Bush and Karl Rove. Bush was preparing to run for governor of Texas and was interested in the policy implications of Olasky's work. Olasky became an advisor. The following year, William Bennett also began talking about *The Tragedy of American Compassion*. Bennett would call it "the most important book on welfare and social policy in a decade. Period." In December 1994—after an election in which Bush won the governor's mansion and Republicans took Congress—Bennett gave a copy of Olasky's book to Newt Gingrich, the man of the moment. Gingrich read the book and touted it all over Capitol Hill.

In 1995 Regnery published *The Tragedy of American Compassion* in paperback, with a foreword by Charles Murray. It became required reading in the conservative movement, and helped influence the harsh welfare bill passed by Congress in 1996. More than anyone, Olasky has helped revive a deeply traditionalist approach to poverty, one that locates the problem strictly at the individual level. Giving handouts to people while asking for nothing in return, Olasky argued, is not compassionate; it is cruel, because it demands no change in behavior and thus enables a person to stay in poverty rather than rise above it. An alternative approach—"compassionate conservatism"—would largely replace government programs with faith-based charities and community groups that "have shown their ability to save and change lives," as Bush put it as governor.[5] By axing antipoverty programs, many Republican lawmakers hope to return America to the earlier, better times that Olasky wrote about.

Olasky has been a frequent target of criticism. But whatever else you might say about him, the truth is that he cares. He is one of many evangelical Christians who feel a biblical mandate to help the needy, and these Americans are *not* part of the disturbing drift in our culture toward a cynical selfishness. When Olasky's son was fourteen, he took the boy on a nationwide tour of inner-city antipoverty initiatives. Not many parents in Berkeley or Cambridge would do something like that. Maybe they'd show their kid an endangered patch of redwood trees. But take him to Camden? I don't think so. Olasky and his wife also adopted an African American child.

A number of Olasky's views are surprisingly consonant with ideas on the left. In particular, Olasky is right that people must be empowered to get out of poverty and that social programs that shuffle them through large bureaucracies won't achieve this goal. Activist groups like ACORN and the Industrial Areas Foundation have been saying as much for decades, as have inner-city faith leaders. And they've acted on this belief, founding thousands of community-building organizations that advance local, decentralized solutions and a philosophy of self-help. Ironically,

though, it is conservatives who have brought empowerment into national policy debates. "Real change in our culture comes from the bottom up, not the top down,"
declared George W. Bush in a 1999 speech heavily shaped
by Marvin Olasky—with just a dash of Saul Alinsky.
When was the last time you heard a Democratic pol say
something like that?

Olasky's focus on the spiritual dimensions of poverty is
also anything but fringe right-wing thinking. A basic
premise of modern psychology is that a person's success is
not governed by material conditions alone. If the dysfunc-
tional rich can slide downward, as we always love to hear,
so too can the self-actualized poor struggle upward. Put a
liberal on Fox News and they'll box themselves into a
blame-the-economy take on poverty. Put them in a policy
seminar and they may tout therapeutic strategies to help
the poor change their lives. (Depression, for instance, is a
major obstacle for women trying to get off welfare.) Put
them in charge of a wayward nephew barely scraping by
and upping the minimum wage won't be their top idea for
helping the kid. A kick in the pants may come to mind
first.

You needn't agree with Olasky to see that any smart
antipoverty strategy must attack both structural and
individual-level causes. Liberals are right to put more
weight on structural issues, especially in this global age, but

they aren't helping their cause by getting sucked into either-or debates.

Finally, who can object to Olasky's insistence that ordinary citizens should help their fellow Americans through tough times? In *The Tragedy of American Compassion*, Olasky argues that pre–New Deal charity worked because it relied heavily on volunteers and tried to involve families and communities in helping people. In contrast, most Americans today have gotten used to thinking about poverty as someone else's problem. We subcontract our compassion to government agencies or the United Way, leaving the job of fighting poverty to "professionals." This is a recipe for failure, to the extent that empowering those who are poor hinges in part on connecting them to the mainstream currents of America—that is, to the lives the rest of us lead. Overcoming deep divides of race and class is key.

Modern antipoverty programs, for all their good intentions, make it easier in some ways for Americans to ignore the less fortunate and slip into self-involvement. As Olasky observes, "We like the way a welfare system, corrupt and inefficient though it is, removes the burden of basic material care from our conscience."[6] If the blame for poverty lies with "society," what can each of us possibly do in our daily lives to make the problem go away? Only government, we've been told, can deal with the complex factors that keep so many people poor. Some social programs push Americans to open their hearts and make personal commitments; most do not.

This doesn't mean that government antipoverty programs have failed. Far from it. The New Deal and the Great Society dramatically cut poverty rates, especially among the aged, and the Earned Income Tax Credit—expanded under Clinton—now lifts nearly five million Americans out of poverty each year. With more generous spending on existing programs, along with a higher minimum wage, we could lift millions more Americans out of poverty. We could do it tomorrow, and we should. This is different, though, from inciting a war on poverty that would push back against a culture of self-interest and get more of us working to empower fellow citizens.

Most people have a hunger to help others. Empathy is a natural emotion, and research by positive psychologists such as Martin Seligman shows that helping others gives us more happiness than self-indulgent activities like shopping or eating out.[7] But it's also scary to get involved in someone else's troubled life. While many people will do tame volunteer work, such as serving the poor at a soup kitchen, most of us will run in the other direction as soon as we are asked to get more enmeshed. A vast social service bureaucracy gives us an excuse to run.

Take my acquaintance with Clive, a homeless man who hung out a few blocks from my apartment in Manhattan during the late 1990s. I got to know Clive because I walked by his spot every day. He was a biracial man in his late thirties with blue eyes and a receding hairline. I gave him money sometimes, and then I started to stop and chat, to see how he was doing. Clive was typical of a lot of homeless men in New York. He had a substance abuse problem that mixed with a mild mental illness of some kind. He also had a leg injury that left him with a bad limp. His hands were swollen, his fingers rubbery. He got by on a small Supplemental Security Income disability check, as well as by panhandling and taking odds jobs. Clive's parents were dead and he had a sister of whose whereabouts he was unsure. I've never met anyone so alone in the world. The saving grace of his bleak life was that he didn't sleep on the sidewalk; he had a room at a single-room-occupancy hotel on Fourteenth Street.

Clive was a sweet man with a gentle way about him. I enjoyed seeing him in the morning, and sometimes on the way home. Often he asked me if I had any jobs for him, and one day he seemed particularly intent on finding work. It turned out he had lost the room at the SRO and was sleeping on the steps of a church around the corner from my building. If he made some money, he might be able to get his room back. I didn't have a job for Clive, but I asked him how he had lost his room. He told me that his disability check had been cut off because of some snafu. To get it restarted, he needed to go to various social service agencies and fill out forms. Jumping through all these hoops was not easy. He needed help with that, and he needed work.

I thought about Clive a lot after he lost his room. I saw him bedded down on the church steps some nights, huddled with the other regulars. The weather was cold and in the morning he was often coughing as he jangled the change in his cup. He looked terrible. The more I thought about him, the more I wanted to do something. I had a phone and an Internet connection. Surely I could cut through whatever red tape was holding up his checks.

So finally I asked Clive if I could help. He didn't think so; a social worker was now handling his case. He hinted at a Byzantine bureaucratic struggle underway, one that was obviously best left to a seasoned professional.

Okay, scratch that idea for being helpful. Until the checks started flowing again, I could think of only one other thing I could do for Clive that would make a difference in his life—a major difference. I could let him sleep on my couch. It was soft and warm, and only about a hundred yards away from the frozen slab of concrete where he currently slept. At the very least, I could invite Clive over to take a bath. He certainly could use one. I imagined how nice it would feel for him to escape the harsh weather and recline back in the tub, soaking his weary limbs in the hot water. It wouldn't be any real trouble for me. Maybe I could help Clive get some better clothes, too. A trip to Daffy's wouldn't exactly bust my bank account. If he was bathed and dressed well, odd jobs might not be so hard to come by.

Did I ever do any of this? No. It seemed too risky to "get involved." I also felt odd about trying to get that close, as if it would violate both Clive's boundaries and mine. Yet a century ago, as Olasky points out, one charity strategy was to have volunteers each take a needy person into their home and help them turn their lives around. Maybe this isn't realistic today—although our houses sure are bigger—but more real human engagement makes a lot of sense. To their credit, Olasky and other antipoverty crusaders on the religious right are moving against the insular, self-protective currents of our time.

All that said, it's too bad Olasky didn't stick to writing forgettable books about the media.

The basic problem with Olasky's moral vision is that it is limited and naïve. While the left is getting more focused on battling poverty by empowering individuals and communities, the right has only grown more dismissive of structural causes—even as those causes become an ever bigger part of the problem. Traditionalists like Olasky won't admit what they are up against. They occupy a mental space where there is no room for pension defaults or plant closings or Blue Cross family premiums rising to $25,000—much less fiber optic networks that lead straight from America's heartland to call centers in Bangalore. They can't see, or won't see, just how much the ever harsher rules of economic competition stand at odds with the basic values of human kinship.

IF YOU WANT to understand the gap between the real world and Olasky world, one good place to start is at the Birkdale Golf Club in Charlotte, North Carolina. There, on a recent May afternoon, a charitable organization called Friendship Trays sponsored its eleventh annual spring golf benefit. HELP DRIVE AWAY HUNGER! read a flyer for the event.

Friendship Trays is a nonprofit organization that has been around for thirty years. It delivers more than seven hundred meals a day to the elderly and people with disabilities in the Charlotte area. The meals come once a day, at lunchtime. While most of us take for granted the ability to heat up a can of Campbell's or make some pasta, this can be a daunting task for a ninety-year-old arthritic woman or someone with advanced multiple sclerosis. There are millions of such people in America, and a vast network of charitable organizations, backed in part by government money, works to keep them alive. Meals on Wheels is the best known of these.

It is hard to imagine a more deserving group than those who can't physically care for themselves, much less hold a job. There is simply no argument for denying these people the food they need to survive. Right?

Since its founding in 1976, Friendship Trays has grown from a handful of volunteers that served six meals a day to a major operation with a special kitchen and warehouse space. Dozens of local churches fund the organization. Area businesses donate money and food. Twelve hundred volunteers help deliver the meals. Friendship Trays is a showcase of effective charity.

It's not effective enough, though. At the time of the golf tournament, Friendship Trays had 135 people on its waiting list. If more people knew about the organization or could swallow their pride enough to ask for help, the demand would be much greater. The goal of the golf benefit was to raise enough money to eliminate the waiting list. A player who gave $2,500 would be called a "Best Friend"; one who donated $800 would be a "Good Friend." All players got a golf shirt, some golf balls, and a boxed lunch.

The benefit was a success, as it had been in years past. But is wasn't so successful that it got rid of the waiting list. Not by a long shot.

Stop for a moment to think about this. In a major city in the wealthiest country in the world—a country so rich that over seven million families have second homes—a respected charity must beg constantly for the resources it needs to feed the most vulnerable of all people, only to fall short.

Charlotte, by the way, is not just any city in America. It is often called "the City of Churches" because it has so many houses of worship—about seven hundred of them.

Billy Graham got his start here, and Jim Bakker started the PTL Club in the city. These days Charlotte is home to dozens of megachurches.

When I arrived in Charlotte, I drove from the airport on Billy Graham Parkway and then followed a tree-lined avenue toward downtown, noticing another church every mile or so. All the major denominations are here: Baptists, Methodists, Lutherans, Episcopalians, Presbyterians, Seventh Day Adventists, Catholics. There are even five mosques in the city. While churches ring the city, along with upscale leafy neighborhoods, new office buildings rise from its center. Charlotte is the second biggest banking center in the United States. Bank of America has its headquarters downtown, as does Wachovia. A half million people now live in Charlotte, and they are doing better than most Americans; median income is well above the national average.

Charlotte would seem to be ideally suited to Olasky's vision of faith-based compassion. It has all the ingredients for success: lots of churches, plenty of money, and numerous charities. At the very least, you'd think hunger would be under control. There are few clearer charitable mandates in most religions than to feed the hungry and, in fact, it is hard to imagine a more straightforward act of moral goodness than providing food to a fellow human being in need. There is also no easier way to help someone. Finding a person a job or a home is complicated; filling their stomach is not. While conservative denominations frown on feeding those who are able-bodied yet idle, there is not much debate about giving food to those who can't work, or those who do work yet don't make enough money to feed their children.

So what exactly does it take to keep hunger at bay in a place like Charlotte? And why is there so much hunger here to begin with?

I took up these concerns in a visit with Beverly Howard, who runs the largest food bank in Charlotte, an outfit called Loaves & Fishes. The organization was founded in 1975 and drew its name from a biblical story in which Jesus fed five thousand hungry people. Loaves & Fishes operates out of a Lutheran church and, as with Friendship Trays, scores of other churches contribute food or money to keep it running. It has sixteen food pantries spread around the city and county and fed nearly 70,000 people in 2005. Volunteer labor keeps the place running. "Charlotte has a very strong volunteer tradition," Howard said. "It's still expected that everyone is involved in supporting one helping organization or the other."

When people turn to Loaves & Fishes for assistance, they get one allotment of groceries for a week, with twenty-one meals for each household member. Howard showed me the grocery list, which mostly consisted of canned foods: tuna, soup, fruit, beans, and so on. Healthy food—while it lasts. The organization's rules are stringent: You need a referral from a social worker or a pastor, and you can get groceries only once every two months. "We don't want anyone to become dependent on us," Howard says.

Howard told me the story of a young couple that came in recently. They were both working at low wages and they had a toddler. Between the costs of transportation and child care, they didn't have much leeway for unexpected expenses. So when fuel prices went up after Katrina, they found themselves coming up short at the end of the month. They came to Loaves & Fishes to bridge the gap.

I wondered about the limit of one visit every two months, and asked Howard what happens when a gap in income was ongoing. She acknowledged that many people are in "a continuing crisis." Typically they went to the Department of Social Services for food stamps. The trouble is that food stamps are means tested, using formulas that are notoriously outdated. As a result, the money that a working couple can expect to get from food stamps might be so paltry that the paperwork isn't worth the trouble. This—along with the stigma people feel about using food stamps—explains why only half of Americans who are eligible for the program participate.[8] (Most antipoverty programs are dramatically underutilized. Far from feeling a deep sense of entitlement, many needy people have too much pride to ask for help, and many others don't know that help exists.)

The young couple with the toddler were not unusual clients for Loaves & Fishes, nor for other food banks across the country. Contrary to myth, 40 percent of poor households in America are headed by a married couple, with one or both of them working.[9] "Most of our clients are the working poor," Howard explained. "They have jobs but don't make ends meet. They work for more than the minimum wage but less than a living wage." A lot of them make $8 or $9 an hour, well over the federal minimum of $5.15. Such money doesn't go very far in Charlotte. One study estimated that two adults with an infant need to both be making at least $11 an hour to cover a bare-bones family budget.[10]

Today only 16 percent of the jobs in North Carolina are still in manufacturing, while low-wage jobs have proliferated. A retail salesperson in North Carolina makes $6.50 on average. Poverty went up in North Carolina during the 1990s even as the state boomed and the unemployment rate fell to 4 percent. Charlotte saw its poverty rate rise by 25 percent during these best of times. Income inequality rose, too. As in other parts of the country, managers and white-collar professionals in North Carolina kept raising their own salaries during the decade. Oftentimes, though, they didn't pay their janitors or mail-room clerks more and, with few strong unions in sight, nobody forced them to do so.[11]

Heroic individual effort and biblical self-discipline aren't much help here. Nor are government programs that get stingier every year. Charities like Loaves & Fishes play an important role in helping the casualties of market failure, but the sad truth is that Americans have become less generous toward the poor in recent years.

This trend shows up clearly in data collected by the Giving USA Foundation. In 2004, individuals and foundations gave $250 billion to charity, which is a lot of money. The catch is that "charity" is defined very broadly. The lion's share of this giving went to the people's own churches, while the next biggest category was the college they attended. Another popular recipient of largesse is local arts organizations.

The amount of money that goes to "human service" organizations that help needy strangers accounts for only about 10 percent of all charitable giving, and this amount has been dwindling. Giving USA data show that donations to human service groups have fallen for the last three years straight, dropping by 13 percent. Meanwhile, you may have noticed that some rich person's name is affixed to more campus buildings and concert halls and museum wings. My favorite story is the one about a billionaire who recently gave $165 million to a university—on the condition apparently that every cent be invested back into a hedge fund that he controls. Donations like that are as tax deductible as money that goes to the Salvation Army. The dominant message of today's culture—feather thy own nest first—has finally shown up in the nonprofit sector's bottom line.[12]

THE CONSERVATIVE RAP on poverty, with its focus on individual responsibility, has now framed social policy debates for a generation. For as long as we can remember, we've been told that help will only hurt, a view that happens to align with growing temptations to focus inward. The more we assume the worst about poor people, the less we have to worry about them. Blaming the victim is simply more convenient, which might be one reason that the ideas of Charles Murray and Marvin Olasky found such a receptive audience during the 1980s and '90s—decades in which selfishness was celebrated as never before.

Knowing all this, I can fathom how we might rationalize withholding food from the hungry. Perhaps they don't deserve that free bag of groceries or that thirty bucks a month in food stamps. Or even if they do deserve help, maybe they'd be better off without it.

Surely, though, nobody can find an excuse for beating up on people with disabilities—or can they?

Across town from Loaves & Fishes is the Program for Accessible Living (PAL), an organization that helps the mentally and physically disabled to live as self-sufficiently as possible. PAL belongs to the national network of Independent Living Centers. The Centers were set up in the 1970s and 1980s as part of a paradigm shift away from treating people with disabilities as helpless and toward a philosophy of empowerment and independent living. They try to tear down the many barriers that stop people with disabilities from having an apartment, holding a job, and otherwise taking care of themselves. Public investment in the Centers pays for itself many times over by keeping these Americans out of expensive institutions and nursing homes. Conservatives should love this stuff.

When I visited PAL, a paraplegic greeted me at the front desk and summoned Julia Sain, the group's executive director. Sain has been with PAL for years and has a formidable job. PAL covers four counties, but Sain has a staff of only eleven people. And over the years, there has been less and less funding for PAL's work. Independent Living centers have been receiving money through the U.S. Department of Education since 1980. It isn't much money; in fact, the amount is so small that it's known among budget wonks as "decimal dust." No matter; ILC funding has still been targeted for cuts. After years of growth through the 1980s, the centers have seen their funding steadily fall. One result is that in many parts of the United States there are no centers to advocate on behalf of people with disabilities. Only thirty-three out of one hundred counties in North Carolina are covered by ILCs.

Like a lot of those who work in social services, Sain manages to get by with limited resources. What troubles her most isn't the erosion of the Independent Living Centers, it is the decimation of key government supports— particularly in the housing area—that allow people with disabilities to live self-sufficiently. When Sain first came to work for PAL, Section 8 vouchers were available to help cover the cost of renting an apartment. Another program, Section 811, also made a big difference. Such assistance is critical, since it allows people with disabilities to get out into the mainstream flow of society.

During the Reagan years the money started to dry up, as funding for Section 8 was frozen or cut. Sain said, "By the early 1990s, there was a five-year wait for vouchers." At the same time, the rental market in Charlotte got much tighter and more expensive. "Our clients couldn't afford to pay the gap," she said, even the ones with jobs. And if their only source of income is Supplemental Security Income, as is the case for many people with disabilities, forget it; an apartment is out of the question.

About four million disabled Americans get an SSI check every month from the government. Many have no source of income beyond SSI and no ability to earn more money. Almost three million people on SSI have severe mental impairments. If they can work, the SSI program encourages that by allowing them to keep some of their monthly check in addition to outside earnings. SSI is widely credited with helping to reduce the number of people confined to institutions over the past few decades, with huge savings to taxpayers.[13] It's hard to think of a more vital government program, and beyond feeding the hungry, there may be no better moral measure of a society than how it treats its citizens with disabilities. Any civilized nation would afford such people a basic level of dignity and security.

Not America. We deliberately keep many people with disabilities in a state of constant deprivation. In 2005, the SSI benefit for an individual with no other source of income was $579 a month, which is below the poverty line. Such money is almost comically inadequate, especially as far as housing goes. An entire SSI check isn't enough to cover the average cost of a one-bedroom apartment in many cities, Charlotte included.[14]

So what happens when housing vouchers disappear and SSI checks amount to pocket change? Bad things. People with disabilities who would rather care for themselves often end up in nursing homes, with Medicaid picking up a tab that can run to $60,000 a year. "At least it's a way to get a roof over your head," Sain said. Another option is to live with aging parents or in a run-down boarding home. Or one can end up on the street. A recent national study found that "millions of the lowest-income people with disabilities have no choice but to live in untenable circumstances."[15]

Given all the conservative talk nowadays about empowerment, it was no surprise when the Bush administration unveiled a "New Freedom Initiative for People with Disabilities" in 2001. This is certainly a group eager to practice Olaskyism. What was surprising, however, is that the administration later turned around and proposed some of the deepest budget cuts ever to programs that foster self-sufficiency. Its 2006 budget called for a 50 percent decrease in funding for Section 811, the one program specifically designed to help people with disabilities find housing. It also proposed to close all the regional offices of the Rehabilitation Services Administration, an agency that helps people with disabilities enter the workforce. As well, it called for cutting in half the budget of another key employment program at the Department of Labor. And, in one further slap at the dream of independent living, the Administration proposed to whack all funding for a special program that helps people with disabilities obtain the "assistive technology" they need to hold certain jobs.

Not all of these cuts were enacted by Congress in 2005—although there is always next year, and the year after that.

Federal budget cuts have a cascading effect. Needs that were once funded by Washington get pushed onto the states, but many states are also strapped. So they push responsibilities onto counties, which don't have enough money either.

The result? "It's all come down to the faith-based community," said Julia Sain, about the trend in North Carolina. "The churches are asking for money all the time."

Sain is a member of one of the Methodist churches in Charlotte and is giving more money than she used to. It is beginning to irk her, though, that religious people like herself are being asked to assume more public responsibilities, and yet it's still illegal to hold prayer in school or to post the Ten Commandments in a courthouse. That seems wrong to Sain. If government is going to shrink, then religion should have more say. Doesn't that make sense?

Maybe it does. And maybe that's not an accidental result of the kinds of cuts favored by conservative lawmakers.

ANY OF US COULD be in a wheelchair tomorrow, and most of us will grow old. If these conditions spell disaster, it's hard to feel empowered to take risks. The temptation instead is to follow the safest route, however much it diminishes your dreams or sells short your potential. In the first few decades after the Great Depression, when the specter of utter destitution was fresh in the national psyche, extreme risk avoidance was common. I don't think we want to go back in that direction. Individual freedom and collective responsibility are two sides of the same coin.

For starters, America should dedicate itself to eliminating poverty among the elderly and people with disabilities. The easiest way to do this is to raise SSI payments and minimum Social Security benefits. These should be pegged not to the archaic federal poverty threshold, but to the real cost of living where a recipient lives. If you're a person with a disability living in Charlotte, you should get enough from SSI to afford an apartment and other basics there. Ditto if you're a widow on Social Security. Again, these ideas are expensive. Are they expensive compared to Bush's tax cuts to the top 1 percent of households? No. Are they expensive compared to the tax breaks that now subsidize 401(k)s for wealthier Americans? No.

The federal government is broke and will be even deeper in the hole when the baby boomers start to retire. We will have to make tough choices—choices that will entail some combination of raising taxes and cutting spending. Personally, I fully expect to be paying higher taxes down the line, getting a smaller mortgage deduction, paying more out of pocket when I go on Medicare, and seeing less in Social Security benefits than my parents did. That's okay with me. As we move into the fiscal crisis that lies ahead, we must ask the better-off to do with less in order to uphold the nonnegotiables of a moral society: basic protections for all, especially for those who cannot fend for themselves.

Meanwhile, we must ask more of those who can be independent and help them change their lives. We can do this through more drug treatment programs, so that addiction isn't an obstacle to self-sufficiency. We can do it through community-building initiatives that bring jobs, housing, bank accounts, and hope to poor neighborhoods. We can do it by enforcing antiredlining laws, so people in all neighborhoods have the capital they need to succeed. We can do it through a higher minimum wage and expanded access to college. We can do it by preventing unwanted pregnancies, by helping young people make better marital decisions, by helping marriages succeed, and by keeping fathers involved in the lives of their children. The truth is that we know more than ever about how to help people transform their lives and rise out of poverty. Some solutions focus on changing personal behavior while others provide more access to opportunity and better rewards for work. Many of the best solutions have been developed not by government agencies but by local community groups.

America may be the wealthiest country in the world, but we have come to take poverty for granted. The poor will always be with us, we seem to believe, and there's nothing we can do about that. This is wrong. Other wealthy countries don't have the poverty rates we do. Plenty of ideas are out there for ending poverty, many of which can win support on both the left and the right. What's needed now is the political will and a greater scale.

We may not have won the last war on poverty. There is every reason to believe we can win the next one.

CHAPTER EIGHT

The Meaning of Patriotism

NOT LONG AFTER SEPTEMBER 11, AN NFL SAFETY named Pat Tillman left behind a $3.6 million football contract with the Arizona Cardinals to join a very different kind of team, the Army Rangers, making a salary of $17,316 a year. He enlisted with his brother Kevin in what turned out to be a recruiting bonanza for the military. "It's a remarkable story," *Sports Illustrated* commented. "Star athlete walks away from the game in his prime, leaving millions in cash on the table, to put his life at risk in service of his country during wartime."[1]

Remarkable is the right word for what Tillman did, at least in this day and age. Six hundred NFL players fought in World War II, and nineteen died. Five hundred Major League Baseball players also fought in that war. Tillman was the only professional athlete who joined the military after September 11.

Tillman never spoke publicly about his decision. But in an interview shortly after the Twin Towers fell, he commented, "At times like this you stop and think about just how good we have it, what kind of system we live in, and the freedoms we are allowed." Football, Tillman said, is "so unimportant compared to everything that has taken place."[2] In another interview, he said, "My great-grandfather was at Pearl Harbor, and a lot of my family has . . . gone and fought in wars, and I really haven't done a damn thing as far as laying myself on the line like that."[3]

Tillman's friends weren't all that surprised when he joined the military. The guy was eccentric in many ways. In addition to playing pro football, he was working on a master's degree in history. He loved late-night bull sessions about the big questions. He was rolling in money but drove the same old pickup truck he'd had for years. He wore his hair long—long enough that it flowed out from under his helmet. Back in college, at Arizona State, he used to meditate atop a two-hundred-foot light tower above the football stadium. Not long before he joined the Army, he had been offered a $9 million contract with the St. Louis Rams. He turned town this fortune out of loyalty to the Cardinals, a team that paid him one-third as much.

Tillman was on a patrol in southeastern Afghanistan when he was killed during a firefight in April 2004. There was an outpouring of publicity around his death, including a statement from the White House about how Tillman had made the "ultimate sacrifice." The national media flocked to Tillman's funeral in his hometown of San Jose, California. Maria Shriver spoke at the service, as did Senator John Mc-Cain, who said that Tillman offered a "welcome lesson in the true meaning of courage and honor." The Army post-humously awarded Tillman the Silver Star, its second-highest honor. The commendation described how Tillman had died as he led a charge against Taliban positions. Till-man emerged as the single most memorable hero of the grueling wars in Afghanistan and Iraq.[4]

It was later revealed that Tillman had actually been killed by friendly fire after a series of deadly mistakes. The Army had lied to his family and the public about what happened. "I think they thought they could control it," Tillman's father said, "and they realized that their recruit-ing efforts were going to go to hell in a handbasket if the truth about his death got out. They blew up their poster boy." Tillman's mother was even blunter: "They wanted to use him for their purposes. It was good for the adminis-tration. It was before the elections. It was during the prison scandal. They needed something that looked good, and it was appalling that they would use him like that." Subsequently, Tillman's mother revealed that her son de-spised Bush, respected Noam Chomsky, and thought the war in Iraq was illegal.[5]

So goes the state of patriotism in America today, where appearances so often trump reality.

George Orwell, writing in 1945, described patriotism as "devotion to a particular place and a particular way of life, which one believes to be the best in the world but has no wish to force on other people." By this definition, patriotism is alive and well across America. In findings that haven't changed much in decades, vast majorities of Americans agree that the United States has the best system of government in the world and the best quality of life. However, if you apply a more stringent definition—say, a willingness to die for one's country—the picture looks different. While most Americans have long said that they would fight for America, one post-9/11 poll showed that only 40 percent agreed that being patriotic required any sort of personal involvement or effort. Another poll, taken during the flag-flying weeks of October 2001, found that 38 percent of undergraduates would seek to get out of military service if a draft were reinstated.[6]

These days, only a guy who used to meditate atop a lighting tower might choose service over fortune. For most people this choice would be unthinkable. In an era where obligation and duty are nearly forgotten concepts, it rarely occurs to any of us to give over a large part of ourselves to defend the common good—whether that means going to fight in Afghanistan or, at the other extreme, going to prison for an antiwar protest. Sacrifice seems like a strange thing in an age of self-interest.

Meanwhile, the political uses of patriotism keep multiplying, affirming Samuel Johnson's famous remark that patriotism "is the last refuge of scoundrels." Patriotic language and symbols are among the most powerful weapons in the culture war. Karl Rove and others deploy these weapons with a sure hand, much as Lee Atwater so skillfully played the race card. More often than not, Democrats don't have a clue how to respond. They hope a smart salute or a giant flag might do the trick, or perhaps one more study about just how few cargo containers are inspected at our ports.

Data from the World Values Survey and the Environics surveys show that feelings of national pride are consistently most intense among Americans who hold a range of other traditional beliefs. God, country, work, and family are absolutes for these traditionalists. Loyalty to each—and all—forms a moral bottom line and worldview. Patriotism of this sort has little to do with serious debate about how to safeguard U.S. national security. It doesn't even have much to do with past military service. Instead, it is more about devotion to a set of traditional values. A draft dodger who often mentions Jesus is a more credible patriot than a combat hero who isn't so comfortable quoting scripture or who has an uppity wife. Just being from a political party that is supposedly at war with traditional values is enough to call into question your ability to defend America.

This insight explains a lot about politics since Vietnam. Such as why a former fearless combat pilot, George McGovern, is still remembered as a virtual traitor in some parts of America. Or why Ronald Reagan, who sat out World War II in Hollywood, is worshiped as a great patriot. Or why Bush and Cheney, neither of whom served when the call came, could ensnare our troops in the cauldron of Iraq and yet still be seen as more patriotic than a decorated war veteran like Kerry. It explains why the three limbs that Senator Max Cleland left behind in Vietnam could not inoculate him, during the 2002 election, against charges that he was "soft." Or why, during the 2000 presidential primaries, John McCain's five years as a prisoner of war could be used against him by the Bush campaign. It explains the otherwise unfathomable personal attacks on Congressman John Murtha, a veteran and well-known military booster, after he called for a pullout from Iraq.

Rarely has patriotism been deployed so viciously or with such brazen hypocrisy as in recent years. But, of course, anyone who has followed the news lately knows all this. What may be less easy to see is the deeper contradiction in many of today's tributes to patriotism.

SACRIFICING FOR ONE'S country in many ways is an irrational act. If Pat Tillman hadn't become a Ranger, someone else would have been on that patrol in Afghanistan. In a country of 300 million, there is always another person to fight and die in one's place. Even during America's greatest national emergencies, people could—and did—opt out of harm's way. Rich Northerners paid to avoid the draft during the Civil War, and the Union still won. The Allies defeated the Axis powers despite the fact that many men, like Reagan, found a way to evade combat. Today, with push-button warfare and smaller threats, there is even less need to get everyone in uniform. It is easier than ever to enjoy the freedoms of America without assuming the gravest of responsibilities.

Other acts considered patriotic, such as voting or volunteering, also aren't always rational. Is any election decided by one vote? Not on the national level. Will the Red Cross run out of blood if you don't take a moment tomorrow to open a vein? No. Will government cease to function if you don't endure the horror show of modern politics to become a public servant? Nope.

To get people to do any of these things, you need to convince them to elevate the common good above their short-term individual interests. Just waving a flag is not enough. Many people will be strongly tempted to be free riders, letting others bear the burdens and risks of ensuring our collective well-being. In his book *The Intellectuals and the Flag*, Todd Gitlin writes that, in a democracy, "lived patriotism entails sacrifice. The citizen puts aside private affairs in order to build up relationships with other citizens, with whom we come to share unanticipated events, risks, and outcomes."[7] That sounds right to me. It sounds like what happened during World War II and here in New York City, where I live, after the horrific events of 9/11. It sounds like what John F. Kennedy was getting at when he declared, "Ask not what your country can do for you. Ask what you can do for your country."

It also sounds out of step with the market values that now have so much sway.

Laissez-faire thinkers have insisted for decades that what America needs most is a purer pursuit of self-interest. Too often, they have sought to weaken, not strengthen, our bonds with fellow citizens. Forget the great democratic ideal of public education, they've said. Every student should get a voucher to shop around in the private market. Forget progressive taxation, with its quaint notion that those who have more should give more. A flat tax would be "fairer." Forget Social Security, which binds us like no other program to a shared fate. Everyone should gamble alone at the Wall Street casino. And definitely forget about national health insurance systems, whether existing ones like Medicare and Medicaid or imagined ones that would cover everyone. What we need instead are Health Savings Accounts so that each of us can independently squirrel away money for the day that illness strikes.

I suppose an argument can be made on behalf of any of these ideas. What you cannot do, though, is relentlessly demand less public life in favor of more private choice and then turn around and claim the mantle of "patriotism."

As with family life, conservatives want to have it both ways on patriotism. They favor an economic creed that extols individual liberty over sacrifice to others and try to extend this logic to more and more parts of society. Yet somehow they expect Americans to magically draw a line when it comes to select areas, like military service or marriage. The real world doesn't work that way. The chairman of General Motors once said that "the business of America is business." Not quite. But work and business dominate the United States more than any other place on earth. It makes sense that the values that rule from 9 to 5 would decisively shape the rest of our outlook. It makes sense that both patriotism and family would be hard sells in an era where the notion of doing anything for anyone is constantly derided as naïve or counterproductive. If we want more people to act against their immediate self-interest in some spheres, we need to defend this ideal across all spheres.

The impossible conflict between "lived patriotism" and the logic of self-interest is vividly illustrated in the way that Washington has fought recent wars. In the distant past, when the Republicans advocated isolationism and small government, there was a consistency in their position. Old-style conservatives wanted neither adventures abroad nor the collectivist policies and higher taxes that such adventures entailed. Liberal internationalists, in contrast, wanted all sorts of crusades—and the big government that came with them.

Today's conservatives fatally mix these ingredients. They want grand crusades abroad and say they're all for sacrifice. In practice, though, their libertarian principles lead them to oppose the tax expenditures that war entails. The deployments in Iraq and Afghanistan have been financed almost entirely on credit. Congress has appropriated over $250 billion for Iraq alone—every penny of which has been added to the national debt. Much of the war's tab will be picked up by Americans who weren't even born when America rolled into Iraq, and who certainly had no say about it. Nothing like this has ever happened in Washington before. When JFK talked about bearing any burden and paying any price, he wasn't referring to the taxpayers of future generations.

NOWHERE IS THE contradiction of today's Beltway patriotism more troubling than in the shabby treatment of our soldiers and veterans.

In August 2005, President Bush made a whirlwind visit to the San Diego Naval Medical Center. The center is one of the major destinations for wounded soldiers returning from Iraq and Afghanistan. It has state-of-the-art facilities for fitting prosthetics and treating spinal cord injuries. Bush met with the center's staff and several soldiers recovering from combat injuries. He presented a Purple Heart to a young man who had been hit in the chest by rifle fire in Fallujah. Another Iraq casualty greeted Bush from his wheelchair. The president thanked the soldiers for their sacrifice. Later, back in Washington and working on the budget, Bush continued the nasty business of withholding health care from many veterans.

A decade ago Congress passed legislation that affirmed the basic principle that anyone who has served his country should have access to decent health care. Since that time, enrollment in the Veterans Health Administration has grown by 141 percent, while funding has grown by only 60 percent. The result has been a perpetual state of triage at the VHA. "Millions of America's veterans and their families are uninsured and face grave difficulties in gaining access to even the most basic medical care," stated a report by a group at Harvard Medical School. The study was shocking, at least to those who hadn't followed the long-standing plight of veterans. It found that backlogs at the VHA left many veterans without such basics as glasses or medication. Over 40 percent of uninsured veterans said they had no usual place to go when sick. Many more than that said they didn't get any preventive care. One-quarter had delayed needed medical care due to cost. These veterans weren't the homeless alcoholics with mental problems that get so much attention in the media. Most were working, and some had two jobs.[8]

Even those veterans who are in the system don't have an easy time getting proper care. Veterans Administration medical centers around the U.S. are struggling to provide services amid budget shortfalls. So it is that a paraplegic veteran in San Antonio couldn't get the special machine he needs to clean a chronic wound, and veterans in Palo Alto had to wait several months for specialty-care appointments, and three operating rooms at a VA medical center in Vermont were closed indefinitely when the air-conditioning system broke, and centers in a number of states in the South have stopped scheduling appointments altogether for some insured veterans.[9]

This crisis is likely to get worse over time. The toll of wounded from the Iraq and Afghanistan wars is now over 15,000, and this number tells only part of the story. Nearly 120,000 military personnel have sought medical care since returning from overseas combat zones. Many veterans have sought help for post-traumatic stress disorder, reflecting the immense psychological cost of these wars. One survey by the Walter Reed Army Institute of Research found that 17 percent of Iraq veterans showed signs of PTSD. That's nearly 100,000 soldiers, a figure not surprising when you consider the other facts turned up by the survey: 95 percent of soldiers who served in Iraq or Afghanistan had been shot at, 68 percent witnessed fellow soldiers being killed or seriously wounded, more than half had killed an enemy combatant, and over a quarter were directly responsible for the death of a civilian.[10]

One reason that these veterans and others won't get the care they deserve is the squeeze caused by the Bush tax cuts. In 2006 alone, those tax cuts total $219 billion. One-third of the cuts went to the top 1 percent of U.S. households. Less than 8 percent went to the bottom 40 percent, from which most members of the U.S. military are drawn. In a familiar story, cuts to services far outweighed any tax savings. Only in this case, we're not talking about money for highways or college tuition; we're talking about meeting a solemn obligation to people who put their lives at risk to protect the rest of us.[11]

Few conservatives would dare make the argument that it's better to give money to millionaires than to provide health care to veterans. Not openly, anyway. Instead, there is a silent dissonance here. Again and again we hear tributes to military duty by the very people who peddle some of the most selfish policies ever seen in the nation's capital. In an age of self-interest, many in the armed forces are there because they didn't have other choices. And the ones who believe that real patriotism means sacrifice? They may find they've been suckered.

Even as we betray those who fight for us, many of our most privileged citizens rationalize away their obligations to America. This is seen not only in the push for further tax cuts for the richest of the rich during a time of war and record deficits—justified by an ever-shifting set of rationales—but also in the growing number of U.S. companies that incorporate offshore to evade taxes. Some two dozen major businesses, including Tyco and the consulting firm Accenture, are officially based in places like Bermuda, though their headquarters remain in the United States. Tyco reportedly saved $400 million in taxes alone in 2001 thanks to its 1997 decision to reincorporate in an overseas tax haven. The trend toward offshore incorporation continued even after September 11, when patriotism was running high, at least among most Americans. One company, Cooper Industries, cut its tax bill by $55 million a year by incorporating in Bermuda less than a year after the terrorist attacks. That didn't stop the company from raking in handsome profits on government contracts with the Defense Department. Another company, Ingersoll-Rand, scooted out to Bermuda just months after the Twin Towers fell—and kept doing a brisk business with all three branches of the U.S. military.[12]

Scores of other U.S. corporations use offshore subsidiaries to achieve largely the same effect. Citigroup has over ninety subsidiaries in offshore tax havens, Bank of America has more than fifty, PepsiCo has nearly thirty.[13]

A 2002 study by Senator Byron Dorgan found that U.S. companies evaded $53 billion in taxes in the previous year by using various pricing schemes involving offshore subsidiaries.[14]

A few years back, there was a brief spurt of attention to these "tax traitors." A 2002 *New York Times* article quoted a partner at Ernst & Young as saying that "just the improvement on earnings is powerful enough that maybe the patriotism issue needs to take a back seat."[15] In the 2004 presidential campaign, John Kerry condemned the "Benedict Arnold CEOs" who dodge taxes by moving overseas. Such name-calling, though, obscures the powerful logic behind incorporating overseas. The effort by a Connecticut company, Stanley Works, to move to Bermuda is a case in point. In justifying the move, which would have saved the company $30 million a year, Stanley said it was just doing the rational thing. "Not only are we disadvantaged against our foreign competitors, but two of our major U.S. competitors, Cooper Industries and Ingersoll-Rand Co., have a significant advantage over Stanley Works because they have already reincorporated," said Stanley chief executive John Trani.[16] Stanley, of course, had no intention of relocating its headquarters from New Britain to Bermuda. It would stay right where it was—and had been for 160 years—keeping the many benefits of being based in America. But it would also have all the tax benefits of Bermudan incorporation. What's not to like about that deal? A strong majority of Stanley's shareholders agreed, voting by a large margin to approve the move in May 2002.

Stanley's reincorporation never happened thanks to heat from politicians and the AFL-CIO. That pressure succeeded because there was a war going on in Afghanistan and also a sudden upsurge in media attention on offshore tax havens. But these are passing conditions. Barring major changes in the law, the logic of moving out of the United States will endure. Patriotism is an intangible value, with no application to quarterly earnings reports. While there once was a time when nonmarket values, such as loyalty to one's workers or local community, carried weight in corporate boardrooms, that time has vanished. The moral imperatives that once surrounded corporate life have been washed away by executive-suite greed, by intensifying global competition, and by the demands of ordinary investors— like you and me—for better returns on our nesteggs. A report by Citizen Works summed up the mood in the title of a report on offshore tax havens: "Sacrifice is for suckers."

The flap over Stanley Works, along with other offshoring efforts, triggered indignation on Capitol Hill. Republican senator Charles Grassley proposed banning government contracts for tax traitors, as did some of his colleagues. Grassley fumed, "We ought to be able to expect American companies to have their heart in America. I think in time of war, you ought to have your heart in America and your properties here and pay your fair share of taxes."[17] Similar sentiments were voiced in newspaper editorials, in opinion magazines, and on radio talk shows. But the whole issue barely broke the surface of public consciousness before the media moved on.

Among the weighty matters it moved on to was the strange case of John Walker Lindh, the young American captured in Afghanistan while fighting for the Taliban. Lindh's story became an obsession of the media, which told a lurid tale about a traitor raised in liberal Marin County north of San Francisco. The elder George Bush referred to Lindh as "some misguided Marin County hot-tubber." The tale seemed to crystallize the connection among the traditional values of God, family, and country. If you were raised in a permissive time and place, with no moral bottom line, it made sense that you would betray the flag.

Later it was revealed that the details about Lindh's background were exaggerated—for instance, his father was a devout Catholic lawyer, not some hippie. No matter. Lindh assumed his place in the pantheon of liberal traitors, and is still invoked regularly by the likes of Sean Hannity and Ann Coulter. All but forgotten, meanwhile, is the fact that scores of U.S. companies are cheating the government out of tens of billions of dollars during a time of war.

Is IT TOO MUCH to ask that patriotism be more than a knee-jerk loyalty test, wrapped up in fealty to traditional values? Not at all. The time of grand causes beyond one's wallet isn't dead yet. It's still possible to nurture the sort of patriotism that's less about God blessing America and more about shared sacrifice. A new patriotism, in fact, may be our best hope for turning around the culture and stemming a rising tide of self-interest, whether in the nation's capital or in the fabric of everyday life. Perhaps it's the stirring ideals of duty, service, and a common higher purpose that can pry people out of their private worlds.

Cultivating these ideals is easier said than done. Quite apart from laissez-faire efforts to separate us from one another, along with other trends that encourage an insular life, America has a longstanding distrust of government.

That's a problem, because a strong public sector is pivotal to any sort of lived patriotism. Government helps us do things together that we can't do alone. It gives us a chance to put aside narrow self-interest and cast our lot with our fellow citizens. Taking a shower with a bunch of other naked people at boot camp is an extreme version of this; there are plenty of mundane ones. I thought about that the other day, when I realized how much money I was paying into Medicare. I'm forty years old and in perfect health, but here I am, shelling out a few thousand bucks every year to cover the medical expenses of old people. I can't say this makes me feel warm and fuzzy, but it does make me feel part of something bigger than my private universe.

In the standard telling, conservatives are the bashers of big government and liberals are its defenders. The truth is more complex. The Great Depression, World War II, the Cold War, and the social upheavals of the 1960s all put the federal government at the center of American society during the twentieth century. That was unusual in our history, and not even September 11 has been enough to carry us back to such times. Moreover, opinion polls across the advanced world show falling trust in most major institutions, including government, since the 1960s. A big reason for this is that people feel more secure than they used to. They're less worried about putting food on the table or being overrun by foreign armies. They don't feel the same need to cede some of their personal autonomy to higher authorities in exchange, say, for physical protection and economic security. They feel more leeway to question and criticize authority. One of the fallouts of more affluence (and fewer world wars) is diminished trust in government.

The right has fanned this trend by proclaiming that the market alone can give us most of what we want, and by endlessly attacking regulation, taxes, and social programs. Reagan said in his inaugural address that government was the problem, not the solution. In his farewell address, he said it was the single biggest threat to liberty. We've been hearing this sort of stuff for thirty years.

But the right hasn't had a monopoly on attacking government. Recent public opinion research by the Frameworks Institute has found that Americans tend to think of government in two negative ways. One way is as a huge bureaucratic monolith—the sullen voice when you call the DMV. That's the government that conservatives complain about incessantly. The second image is of government as a group of self-serving leaders—the people you see on TV. This image is more dominant in the public's mind, according to Frameworks. Both left and right have helped create that image.

It was Timothy Leary, not G. Gordon Liddy, who said, "Question authority." Long before the Whitewater witch hunt, Beltway politicians of all stripes perfected the politics of scandal and programmed the American public to be skeptical of executive-branch authority. Many claims of government deception and abuse of power have come from the left. Such complaints have remained a liberal staple in recent years with incessant talk about the corrupting influence of money on politics and, more recently, the many lies of the Bush Administration as well as its Big Brother impulses. While most of these criticisms have been necessary, they've also fanned cynicism and made it harder to use government to promote an authentic, selfless patriotism. In a related misstep, the left got into the bad habit of demonizing just about anyone in a uniform—especially cops and soldiers. That was a mistake. Disagreeing with a reckless foreign policy or heavy-handed police tactics makes much sense; bashing low-paid public servants makes no sense.

This goes to a larger contradiction. Liberals has been ex-
tolling personal autonomy for four decades—all the while
wringing their hands about people who "bowl alone" or push
to lower taxes or oppose national health insurance. I understand the difference between having the government in my
bedroom and having it in my workplace. But this is America, where libertarianism runs deep. If you try to promote
more individualism in some realms and more collectivism in
others, chances are you'll just get more individualism.

BACK IN EARLY 2004, Alex Garwood was enjoying the
kind of comfortable, inward-directed life that America offers in abundance. Still in his late twenties, he was making
great money at a software company in Silicon Valley. He
lived with his wife and two children in Los Gatos, a town
in the foothills of the Santa Cruz Mountains where the average home costs about a million bucks. Life was good.

Then his brother-in-law and best friend, Pat Tillman,
was killed in Afghanistan.

Within days Garwood decided he would leave his job
and do something to honor Tillman's legacy. Exactly what
took some time to figure out. Eventually, though, working
without pay, Garwood helped to create the Pat Tillman
Foundation and became its executive director. Within
months the group had received hundreds of donations,
some small, some large. Children even sent in coins. In

New York City, two men who had heard about the foundation put together a fundraiser that brought in $30,000. "I think people forget about sacrifice," one of the men told a reporter. The other said that Tillman's "unselfishness is just unprecedented."[18]

The Pat Tillman Foundation is organized around an initiative called Leadership for Action, which seeks to develop the "leaders of our future—inspiring and supporting them as they tackle real social problems." The Foundation talks about fostering "compassion, integrity and conviction." It has funded a two-semester course at Arizona State's business school, where Pat Tillman Scholars learn about leadership and develop service projects in the community.

Alex Garwood has taken a major financial hit to try to get more people to think beyond themselves. That's impressive. But these days, leadership programs—and would-be leaders—are more common on college campuses than guys with long hair. So are community service programs. Forget lazy afternoons on the quad with a Frisbee. Kids today are just as overscheduled in college as they are in elementary school, and showing they can lead is one of the things keeping them so busy.

But lead where? To what purpose? Many of the leadership initiatives are vague about the problems that need to be solved by tomorrow's leaders, much less the causes of these problems. The Pat Tillman Foundation, for instance, never actually identifies any of the social ills that it hopes to address. And it is a rare leadership effort that critiques the market values that counsel against service to others or generate so many of our social problems. Such thinking is off the table in most of America. While many universities have embraced the drive for social equality that arose out of 1960s, cultural critiques of capitalism stand largely forgotten. Chalk up as another reason why liberals struggle to forge an authentic patriotism: They no longer challenge the main force turning us inward. We may or may not all be multiculturalists now, as sociologist Nathan Glazer has suggested, but certainly we are all free marketeers.

This is a major obstacle to a real patriotism, but maybe one we can work around over time. While young people are tuned out of national politics and current events to a shocking degree, many are very tuned in to community life. They think locally about change by starting a mentoring program or a literacy initiative or by building houses for Habitat for Humanity. Some research on the Millennials, or Generation Y, suggests that they are less individualistic than Generation X or the boomers. As Neil Howe and William Strauss write in *Millennials Rising*, "They're cooperative team players. From school uniforms to team learning to community service, they are gravitating toward group activity. According to a recent Roper survey, more teenagers blamed 'selfishness' than anything else when asked, 'What is the major cause of problems in this country?' Unlike Gen Xers, they believe in their own collective power." They also trust government more than have past generations.[19]

If this is even partially true (other research offers a less sanguine picture), efforts like the Pat Tillman Foundation may be operating in fertile ground and could help move our culture away from a celebration of self-interest. Perhaps it's the Millennials who will help revive the anachronistic notions of sacrifice and service to the common good. Maybe they'll take to heart Martin Luther King, Jr.'s declaration that "a man who won't die for something is not fit to live." And while they don't yet think structurally about the problems of capitalism, maybe they will later, as their small-bore volunteerism runs up against systemic obstacles.

Maybe. But if a new selfless ethos is to take root and spread, it will need to be fueled by larger efforts to teach— and reward—the values of service and sacrifice.

How DO WE do this?

Bringing back the draft is a common idea. However, weaponry and warfare is a lot more complicated than it used be—too complicated for draftees to master in a year or two. An all-volunteer army, with soldiers in for at least several years, is far more effective. As for some sort of compulsory national service, in which people have a choice over how they serve, it is too easy to see this turning into a joke. Rich kids will work to stem erosion on the Cape Cod National Seashore; poor kids will work to stop infiltration on the Iraq-Syria border.

Voluntary service programs, particularly AmeriCorps, make more sense. Our goal should be to so dramatically scale up this effort so that it comes close to being a system of national service. About a half million young people have gone through AmeriCorps since 1994, and research shows that these alumni continue to make a contribution afterward. Many end up as teachers or police officers or social workers. They also are likely to follow current events and be civically engaged in their community. Even taking into account the self-selecting bias of those who join AmeriCorps, it is clear that the program has a major impact on people. The problem is scale. Three million kids graduate from high school every year; AmeriCorps at its height has never accepted more than 75,000 applicants. Quadrupling the program, to reach at least 10 percent of high school graduates, would be a sensible goal. A much larger pool of AmeriCorps graduates could help form the backbone of a more committed citizenry, and perhaps lead us into a different cultural moment.

This isn't a liberal pipe dream. In 2001, not long after September 11, Senators John McCain and Evan Bayh introduced the bipartisan Call to Service Act that would have expanded AmeriCorps to 250,000 participants. Similar legislation was introduced in the House of Representatives.

That effort failed—we got tax cuts on dividends instead—but the idea is still out there, along with the potential for bipartisan support.

Another solution is to increase the rewards for those people who sacrifice for the common good. If it's impractical to demand service from every citizen, let's at least take better care of those who take care of us. In particular, we should better reward military service and use this institution to increase economic mobility. We need to channel the spirit of the 1944 GI Bill of Rights, which stands as one of the most effective pieces of social legislation in U.S. history. It was a home run because its benefits were predicated on the notion of reciprocity. Those who sacrificed were rewarded with free tuition for higher education and low-interest loans to buy a home or start a business. These benefits were some of the most generous ever provided by a government program, but they were contingent on working to improve yourself. Eight million Americans went to school on the GI Bill, a major reason for the huge expansion of the middle class during the postwar period.

The GI Bill still exists, but its benefits aren't as generous as in the past and, in many ways, the prognosis is poor for the hundreds of thousands of Americans who have already served in Afghanistan and Iraq. Many of these veterans have mental problems caused by combat. Others have financial difficulties brought on from being overseas. Some have even lost their homes. If the problems of veterans are left unaddressed, the stateside human cost from recent wars could steadily mount in the decades ahead—just as the toll from the Vietnam War still reverberates through our communities. It will affirm the lesson that sacrifice is for suckers.

We need a "GI Bill of Rights for the Twenty-first Century," as some have suggested, that would expand access to mental health care, education, and loans for homes and small businesses. Those who join the military right after high school and serve twenty years will barely be forty by the time they retire. They'll have plenty of time to seek a secure place in the middle class and raise children that will do better than they did. They should have what they need to move in that direction. If you sacrifice to defend the American Dream, you and your children should be able to achieve it.

Only a small percentage of Americans will ever go through the military or even a greatly expanded Ameri-Corps. To foster stronger bonds among citizens, those in the moral center should seek to strengthen a variety of institutions that operate outside the market and promote what journalist Mickey Kaus has called "civic equality." These include public schools, parks, and arts organizations, public transportation, and key social insurance programs—like Medicare—that cement links between the old and the young, and the rich and the poor. Fostering stronger intergenerational ties is especially critical. Things could get very ugly as the largely white boomers retire and an increasingly nonwhite work force is asked to support them in old age amid vast fiscal shortfalls. A better future would enmesh all these Americans in each other's lives. For instance, why not open up an expanded AmeriCorps to retirees?

Civic equality also means bolstering our democracy. We need to get big money out and more ordinary people in, as well as to make elections more competitive, so that the shared rituals of civic life no longer seem like a charade. This is not just a liberal idea. In the 1990s, Ross Perot and millions of his followers almost upended the two-party system with an agenda that hinged in large part on political reform. These demands may be latent right now, but those voters haven't gone away. They may be a key to a new governing majority.

In the end, greater civic equality will hinge on more economic equality. It was FDR who said that "freedom is no half-and-half affair. If the average citizen is guaranteed equal opportunity in the polling place, he must have equal opportunity in the market place." Supreme Court Justice Louis Brandeis may have said it better: "We can have concentrated wealth in the hands of a few or we can have democracy. But we cannot have both."

Conclusion

I N THE WAKE OF THE 2004 ELECTION, SOMEONE e-mailed me a political cartoon that showed how pre–Civil War fault lines mirror today's divisions. The 2004 red states were many of the same ones that held slaves, while the blue states formed the core of the Union, circa 1861.

Maybe you saw the same cartoon. Or maybe, if you live in a place like Brooklyn or Cambridge or Seattle, you heard the smug banter about just how backward life is in the red states, what with their higher levels of obesity, incest, and illiteracy. Maybe you heard some half-serious talk about moving to Canada. Or maybe you saw an advertisement for THINK BLUE hats and wristbands. Since the election, more than 150,000 such wristbands have been sold. They are still selling. The THINK BLUE products are manufactured by

Clothing for the American Mind, a Los Angeles–based company that describes itself as "supporting and articulating progressive values through fashion."

I don't see how this sort of thing does any good. The hardcore traditionalists who have monopolized the values debate only make gains when we all focus on the "culture war." In the current conflict, the edge goes to the right—not because Americans in the middle share their agenda, but because an extremist moral bottom line is more attractive than no bottom line.

As I have argued in this book, the tug-of-war between traditionalism and modernism often misses the point. It is an unfettered free market—and the self-interested mindset it fans—that now poses the gravest threat to the morals of our society. The Cares on both sides of the partisan divide need to recognize this and refocus their attention. I hope that in time the religious right will end their alliance with probusiness libertarians and get serious about protecting "family values" from an economic system that is increasingly at war with these values. Ordinary evangelicals are not always in sync with their leaders, and perhaps they will come to push those leaders away from an unequivocal embrace of the market. For now, though, I'm not holding my breath.

That leaves the job up to others. In particular, liberals must again find their gift for critiquing the moral downsides of capitalism in ways that are in sync with America's

unique political and cultural conditions. As William Galston has rightly suggested, "We must begin from where we
are. We must go with—not against—the American grain."
I hope this book has suggested some useful ways forward
and that a longer conversation, and much new thinking,
lies ahead.

Ultimately, the appeals on behalf of a new moral center can't be anodyne or technocratic. They must be visceral.
Changing the culture is as important as changing policy—
in fact, we can forget about new policies without a change
in people's consciousness and lifestyles. As the Italian the-
orist Antonio Gramsci noted long ago, you must capture
the culture first if you hope to capture political power. The
conservative movement has embraced this insight, just as
the left did in the 1960s, which is one reason why they
have been so successful. Evangelical megachurches offer
some of the strongest forms of community that now exist
in America. And in many ways, the policy agenda of the religious right is simply an extension of a broader call for
moral renewal that is intensely personal.

Those in the moral center must get personal, too. The
issues I've talked about in this book are not abstract; they
affect our daily life as we are hammered by economic
stresses and an increasingly crass culture. Most people already have personal conversations about values, particularly parents. The trick is to tap into these conversations
and connect them to policy debates. We need leaders who

can do this, and who can talk about individual choices and structural problems at the same time. Let's hear calls for better policies *and* better behavior. And let's pay attention not just to innovative programs that solve problems, but also to real people who are modeling the values that we believe in. We should talk about these people and why we admire them, making their stories part of a broader narrative. And, if we really believe in a moral center that better balances freedom and responsibility, we should make changes in our own lives, and push our friends and family to do the same.

Once upon a time it was said that "the personal is political." Times are different, but this truth endures.

notes

Chapter One: What's Really Wrong

1. "Issues in the 2000 Election: Values," *The Washington Post*/Kaiser Family Foundation/Harvard University, September 2000; "Disapproval of GOP Congressional Leaders, But Democrats Fare No Better," Pew Research Center for the People and the Press survey conducted by Princeton Survey Research Associates International. March 17–21, 2005.

2. Jeffrey Stonecash, *Class and Party in American Politics* (Boulder, CO: Westview Press, 2000); Larry Bartels, "What's the Matter with *What's the Matter with Kansas*," February 2006; William Galston and Elaine C. Kamarck, *The Politics of Polarization*, The Third Way Middle Class Project, October 2005, p. 14.

3. See: "American Voters Say Urgent Moral Issues Are Peace, Poverty And Greed," Zogby International, November 12, 2004. On the Catholic vote, see: "Reclaiming the Catholic Vote," Democracy Corps, March 2005. On health care and minorities, see: "Issues in the 2000 Election: Values," *The Washington Post*/Kaiser Family Foundation/Harvard University, September 2000.

4. Michael Adams, *Fire and Ice: The United States, Canada and the Myth of Converging Values* (Toronto: Penguin Books Canada, 2003. For a more in-depth analysis of this data, see: *Roadmap for a Progressive Majority*, American Environics, September 2005.

5. ABC News/*Washington Post Poll*. December 15–18, 2005, as reported by www.pollingreport.com. And: "Politics and Values in a 51%–48% Nation," Pew Research Center for the People and the Press, January 2005, p. 5.

6. A good summary of the many polls on the Schiavo case can be found at www.pollingreport.com.

CHAPTER TWO: FAMILY MATTERS

1. Robert L. Borosage and Stanley B. Greenberg, *The Next Agenda* (Washington, D.C.: Campaign for America's Future, 2001). See introduction.

2. "Life's Work: Generational Attitudes Toward Work and Life Integration," Radcliffe Public Policy Center, 2000, p. 3; "Family Values: Belief in Marriage and Family Life Remains Strong," *ISR Update*, vol. 2, no. 1, University of Michigan, Fall 2002, p. 1.

3. William Bennett, *The Broken Hearth: Reversing the Moral Collapse of the American Family* (New York: Doubleday, 2001), p. 21. For a very different conservative account of what's gone wrong with marriage, one that largely discounts the 1960s, see: James Q. Wilson, *The Marriage Problem: How Our Culture Has Weakened Families* (New York: HarperCollins, 2002).

4. Daniel Bell, *The Cultural Contradictions of Capitalism* (New York: Basic Books, 1996), p. 69.

5. Robert Bork, *Slouching Toward Gomorrah: Modern Liberalism and American Decline* (New York: HarperCollins, 1996).

6. Ronald Inglehart, *Modernization and Postmodernization: Cultural, Economic, and Political Change in 43 Nations* (Princeton, NJ: Princeton University Press, 1997), p. 28.

7. Ibid., p. 40.

8. On gender equality see: "Equal Role for Women," The American Nation Election Studies Guide to Public Opinion, University of Michigan. On

housework, the classic account is Arlie Hochschild, *The Second Shift* (New York: Penguin Books, 1989). On real estate: Stephanie Rosenbloom, "For Men, A Fear of Commitment," *New York Times*, February 12, 2005, Section 11, p. 1.

9. Chen Weihua, "Divorce rate surges across China," *China Daily*, February 15, 2006, p. 33; Peter Foster, "Divorce Soars in India's Middle Class," *The Daily Telegraph*, October 1, 2005, p. 18.

10. Maggie Gallagher and Linda Waite, *The Case for Marriage: Why Married People are Happier, Healthier, and Better off Financially* (New York: Doubleday, 2000); see also: J. Ross Eshleman and Steven Stack, "Marital Status and Happiness: A 17-Nation Study," *Journal of Marriage and the Family*, vol. 60, no. 2 (May 1998), pp. 527–536; and *Why Marriage Matters, Second Edition: Twenty-six Conclusions from the Social Sciences* (New York: Institute for American Values, 2004).

11. Nancy Folbre, *The Invisible Heart: Economics and Family Values* (New York: The New Press, 2001).

12. On early divorce, see: *Cohabitation, Marriage, Divorce, and Remarriage in the United States*, Centers for Disease Control and Prevention, National Center for Health Statistics, July 2002, p. 17; and Pamela Paul, *The Starter Marriage and the Future of Matrimony* (New York: Villard Books, 2002).

13. Paul Asay, "Religious Leaders, Mayor Back Marriage Covenant," *Colorado Springs Gazette*, January 24, 2006.

14. *Cohabitation, Marriage, Divorce, and Remarriage in the United States*, p. 55. "Marriage Dissolutions and Dissolution Rates by County and Region, Colorado Occurrence, 2001," Colorado Department of Public Health and Environment, 2001. See also: "Boulder County" and "El Paso County," U.S. Census Bureau. All data are from 1999 or 2000. In some Colorado counties that are much poorer than El Paso, such as Alamosa County, the divorce rate is even higher. But the correlation between income and socioeconomic status is not exact. The lowest divorce rates in the state are found in the most rural, sparsely populated counties—places with incomes well below the state average, and where few people have gone to college.

15. A 1977 study found that people with few assets and low income were far more likely to get divorced. Another study in 1986 concluded that "the

accumulation of assets substantially reduced the propensity to divorce." A 2004 study found that "the difficulty of staying married increases substantially with levels of economic disadvantage." See: Stephen Bahr, *The Effects of Income and Assets on Marital Instability: A Longitudinal Analysis* (Provo, UT: Brigham Young University, 1977); and A. Booth et al., "Divorce and Marital Instability Over the Life Course," *Journal of Family Issues*, vol. 7, no. 4, December 1986, pp. 421–42; David J. Fein, "Married and Poor: Basic Characteristics of Economically Disadvantaged Married Couples in the U.S.," *Supporting Healthy Marriage*, July 2004. See also: Steven P. Martin, "Growing Evidence for a 'Divorce Divide'? Education and Marital Dissolution Rates in the U.S. Since the 1970s," unpublished paper.

16. "Equal Role for Women," *The American Nation Election Studies Guide to Public Opinion*, University of Michigan; and *Cohabitation, Marriage, Divorce, and Remarriage in the United States*, Centers for Disease Control and Prevention, National Center for Health Statistics, July 2002, p. 2.

17. "Marriage and Divorce Rates by State: 1990, 1995, and 1999–2002," Centers for Disease Control and Prevention.

18. D. Olson, "National Survey of Marital Strengths," Life Innovations, Inc., 2000; and James P. Marshall and Linda Skogrand, "Debt Brought Into Marriage: The Anti-Dowry," Utah State University, May 2003. Other money troubles occur if someone can't find a job. Research confirms what many of us know from experience: even temporary unemployment can poison a relationship pretty quickly. See: Robert Caplan, Richard Price, and Amiram Vinokur, "Hard Times and Hurtful Partners: How Financial Strains Affects Depression and Relationship Satisfaction of Unemployed Persons and Their Spouses," *Journal of Personality and Social Psychology*, vol. 71, no. 1 (1996), pp. 166–79.

19. "Time, Sex, and Money: The First Five Years of Marriage," Center For Marriage And Family, Creighton University, 2000.

20. David J. Fein, "Married and Poor: Basic Characteristics of Economically Disadvantaged Married Couples in the U.S.," Supporting Healthy Marriage Evaluation, Abt Associates, July 2004.

21. Latino wages reported: "The State of Working Colorado 2003," Col-

orado Fiscal Policy Institute, 2004, p. 21; "The State of Housing," Colorado Housing and Finance Authority, 2005.

22. Wayne Baker, *America's Crisis of Values: Reality and Perception* (Princeton, N.J.: Princeton University Press, 2005), p. 62, 77.

23. "Issues in the 2000 Election: Values," Kaiser Family Foundation, September 2000, p. 17; Alan Wolfe, *Moral Freedom: The Search for Virtue in a World of Choice* (New York: W.W. Norton, 2001), p. 225.

24. "What Next for the Marriage Movement?" Institute for American Values, December 16, 2004. See also: Matthew Stagner et al., "Update on a Systematic Review of the Impact of Marriage and Relationship Programs," National Poverty Center, University of Michigan, September 5, 2003.

CHAPTER THREE: SEX AND RESPONSIBILITY

1. Timothy Miller, *The Hippies and American Values* (Knoxville, TN: University of Tennessee Press, 1991). See chapter 3.

2. Richard Godbeer, *Sexual Revolution in Early America: Gender Relations in the American Experience* (Baltimore, MD: Johns Hopkins University Press, 2002).

3. Stephanie Coontz, *The Way We Never Were: American Families and the Nostalgia Trap* (New York: Basic Books, 1992), p. 185.

4. Beth Bailey, *From the Front Porch to the Back Seat* (Baltimore, MD: Johns Hopkins University Press, 1989).

5. Ibid., p. 185. In 1920, Margaret Sanger estimated the number of abortions in the United States at between one and two million, figures echoed by others but impossible to verify. See: Margaret Sanger, *Woman and the New Race* (New York: Brentano's, 1920), chapter 10. A similar estimate is found in Leslie J. Reagon, *When Abortion Was a Crime* (Berkeley: University of California Press, 1997).

6. Alfred Kinsey et al., *Sexual Behavior in the Human Male* (Bloomington: Indiana University Press, 1998); and *Sexual Behavior in the Human Female* (Bloomington: Indiana University Press, 1998).

7. "UF Study: Sexual Revolution Began With 'Silent Generation' of '40s and '50s," University of Florida, November 29, 2004.

8. Rose Kreider and Tavia Simmons, "Marital Status: 2000," U.S. Census Bureau, October 2003, p. 10.

9. Cited in Kristin Luker, *Dubious Conceptions: The Politics of Teenage Pregnancy* (Cambridge, MA: Harvard University Press, 1996), p. 87.

10. David J. Harding and Christopher Jencks, "Changing Attitudes Toward Premarital Sex: Cohort, Period, and Aging Effect," *Public Opinion Quarterly*, vol. 67 (2003), pp. 211–26; John Leo, "The Revolution Is Over," *Time*, April 9, 1984, p. 74.

11. Norval Glenn and Elizabeth Marquardt, "Hooking Up, Hanging Out, and Hoping for Mr. Right," Institute for American Values, 2001.

12. "Teen Sex and Pregnancy," Alan Guttmacher Institute, 1999, p. 1.

13. "A Series of National Surveys of Teens About Sex: Gender Roles," Sex Smarts: Kaiser Family Foundation/*Seventeen*, December 2002.

14. "Teen Sex and Pregnancy," p. 2.

15. "Adolescent Sexual Behavior, II: Socio-Psychological Factors," Advocates for Youth, November 2002, pp. 1–2.

16. "Sex on TV 4," Kaiser Family Foundation, November 2005, pp. 1, 5; Rebecca Collins et al., "Watching Sex on Television Predicts Adolescent Initiation of Sexual Behavior," *Pediatrics*, September 2004, p. 280. The glimmer of good news in the research is that the shows with references to sexual intercourse most watched by teenagers were also the shows most likely to have references to safe sex. See: "Sex on TV 3," Kaiser Family Foundation, 2003, p. 4; and Jane D. Brown, "Mass Media Influences on Sexuality," *Journal of Sex Research*, February 2002. On earlier sex, see: Rebecca Collins et al., "Watching Sex on Television Predicts Adolescent Initiation of Sexual Behavior," *Pediatrics*, September 2004, p. 280. On teen regrets, see for example: *Not Just Another Thing to Do*, survey from the National Campaign to Prevent Teen Pregnancy, June 30, 2000.

17. Michael Cobb and William Boettcher, "Exposure to Misogynist Rap Music and Ambivalent Sexism: Does Eminem's Music Generate Hostility Toward Women?" unpublished paper; Tracy L. Dietz, "An Examination of Violence and Gender Role Portrayals in Video Games: Implications for Gender Socialization and Aggressive Behavior," *Sex*

Roles: A Journal of Research, March 1998, pp. 425–42. See for example: Katharina Lindner, "Images of Women in General Interest and Fashion Magazine Advertisements From 1955 to 2002," *Sex Roles: A Journal of Research*, October 2004.

18. Anne Becker, "Television, Disordered Eating, and Young Women in Fiji: Negotiating Body Image and Identity During Rapid Social Change," *Culture, Medicine, and Psychiatry*, December 2004, pp. 533–59. For a summary of research on media effects of body image, see: "Fact Sheet: Media's Effect on Girls: Body Image and Gender Identity," National Institute on Media and the Family, September 2002. On cosmetic surgery: American Society of Plastic Surgeons, "Briefing Papers: Plastic Surgery for Teenagers," August 2004.

19. On the prevalence of abstinence programs, see: "Sex Education: Politicians, Parents, Teachers and Teens," Alan Guttmacher Institute, February 2001. On public opinion, see: D. W. Haffner et al., "Vast Majority of Americans Support Sexuality Education," *SIECUS Report*, August/September 1999. For the best account of what works in sex education, see: Douglas Kirby, *Emerging Answers: Research Findings on Programs to Reduce Teen Pregnancy, Summary*, The National Campaign to Prevent Teen Pregnancy, May 2001.

20. Lawrence B. Finer and Stanley K. Henshaw, "Estimates of U.S. Abortion Incidence in 2001 and 2002," The Alan Guttmacher Institute, May 18, 2005: "Induced Abortion in the United States," Alan Guttmacher Institute, 2005; and Susan Cohen, "Contraceptive Use is Key to Reducing Abortion Worldwide," *The Guttmacher Report on Public Policy*, October 2003, pp. 7–10. Jim Kessler et al., "The Demographics of Abortion," Third Way, August 2005, p. 6.

21. Cohen, "Contraceptive Use is Key to Reducing Abortion Worldwide," p. 8.

22. Ammie N. Feijoo, "Adolescent Sexual Health in Europe and the U.S.— Why the Difference?" Advocates for Youth, October 2001.

23. For an argument along these lines, see William Saletan, "Three Decades After *Roe*, a War We Can All Support," *New York Times*, January 22, 2006, p. 17.

Chapter Four: Tipper Gore Was Right

1. "Parents, Media and Public Policy: A Kaiser Family Foundation Survey," Kaiser Family Foundation, Fall 2004.

2. "New Concerns About Internet and Reality Shows, Support for Tougher Indecency Measures, But Worries About Government Intrusiveness," Pew Research Center for the People and the Press, April 19, 2005.

3. Robert L. Borosage and Stanley B. Greenberg, "Introduction," *The Next Agenda*, Campaign for America's Future, February 2001.

4. "Merchants of Cool," *Frontline*, 2001.

5. James T. Hamilton, *Channeling Violence: The Economic Market for Violent Television Programming* (Princeton, N.J.: Princeton University Press, 1998), p. 3. See also: Jonathan Rintels and Philip M. Napoli, "Ownership Concentration and Indecency in Broadcasting: Is There a Link," Center for Creative Voices, September 2005, pp. 9–10.

6. "Striking the Balance: Audience Interests, Business Pressures, and Journalists' Values," Pew Research Center for the People and the Press, March 30, 1999.

7. "Industry Totals: TV/Movies/Music," and "Gun Rights: Long-Term Contribution Trends," Opensecrets.org, The Center for Responsive Politics.

8. Joe Eszterhas, "Memo to My Hollywood Friends," *Salon*, August 29, 2000.

9. On kids and books, see: Kevin Nance and Mike Thomas, "The End of Books?" *Chicago Sun-Times*, July 22, 2004.

10. "Generation M: Media in the Lives of 8–18 Year Olds," Kaiser Family Foundation, March 2005, p. 20.

11. Ibid., p. 18.

12. Ibid., p. 24.

13. "Zero to Six: Electronic Media in the Lives of Infants," Kaiser Family Foundation, October 2003.

14. "Key Facts: TV Violence," Kaiser Family Foundation, Spring 2003.

15. See ibid., for a review of the research.

16. On music, see: Craig Anderson et al., "Exposure to Violent Media: The Effects of Songs with Violent Lyrics on Aggressive Thoughts and Feelings," *Journal of Personality and Social Psychology*, 84 (2001), pp. 960–71. On

video games, see: Craig A. Anderson and Brad J. Bushman, "Effects of Violent Video Games on Aggressive Behavior, Aggressive Cognition, Aggressive Affect, Physiological Arousal, and Prosocial Behavior: A Meta-Analytic Review of the Scientific Literature," *Psychological Science*, vol. 12, no. 5 (September 2001), pp. 353–359.

17. David Walsh et al., "Video Game Report Card," National Institute on Media and Family, November 23, 2004, p. 2.

18. Reported in Douglas A. Gentile et al., "The Effects of Violent Video Game Habits on Adolescent Hostility, Aggressive Behaviors, and School Performance," *Journal of Adolescence*, 27 (2004), pp. 5–22.

19. Brad Bushman and Craig Anderson, "Media Violence and the American Public: Scientific Facts Versus Media Misinformation," *American Psychologist*, June/July 2001, pp. 477–89.

20. On what kids read, see: "Tweens, Teens, and Magazines—Fact Sheet," Kaiser Family Foundation, October 2004. On media time, see: "Generation M: Media in the Lives of 8–18 Year Olds," p. 26.

21. Juliet Schor, *Born to Buy: The Commercialized Child and the New Consumer Culture* (New York: Scribner, 2004), pp. 13, 21.

22. "Public Perceptions of Public Broadcasting," Corporation for Public Broadcasting, December 2003.

23. Ibid.

24. Paul Farhi, "A Message Loud and Clear," *Washington Post Weekly Edition*, July 25–31, 2005, pp. 10–11.

25. "Parents, Media, and Public Policy," p. 4.

26. Joel Federman, "Rating Sex and Violence in the Media: Media Ratings and Proposals for Reform," Kaiser Family Foundation, November 2002, p. 10.

CHAPTER FIVE: PUNISHMENT FOR SOME

1. Pamela Manson, "Victims Outraged as Developer Dodges Jail in Fraud Case," *Salt Lake Tribune*, December 10, 2005.

2. Robert Merton, *Social Theory and Social Structure* (New York: The Free Press, 1949), p. 167; and Steven F. Messner and Richard Rosenfeld, *Crime and The American Dream* (Belmont, CA: Wadsworth, 1994), p. 87.

3. Seymour Martin Lipset, *American Exceptionalism: A Double-Edged Sword* (New York: Norton, 1996), p. 48.

4. Quoted in Messner and Rosenfeld, *Crime and the American Dream*, p. 92.

5. "Insurance Fraud," Insurance Information Institute, February 2006.

6. Bruce Western, *Punishment and Inequality in America* (New York: Russell Sage Foundation, forthcoming). See introduction.

7. "The Bush Record on Workplace Health and Safety," American Federation of State, County, and Municipal Employees, May 2004.

8. David Barstow, "U.S. Rarely Seeks Charges for Deaths in Workplace," *New York Times*, December 22, 2003, p. 1. On Moeves case, see also: "OSHA Fines Moeves Plumbing $150,000 for Willful and Serious Violations of Trenching and Excavation Safety Rules," U.S. Department of Labor, Feburary 4, 2005.

9. *Death on the Job: The Toll of Neglect*, AFL-CIO, April 2005, p. 4.

10. Ibid., p. 9.

11. Testimony of David J. Graham, Senate Finance Committee, November 18, 2004. See also: Marc Kaufman, "FDA Official Alleges Pressure to Suppress Vioxx Findings," *The Washington Post*, October 8, 2004, A-23.

12. Alex Berenson, "Evidence in Vioxx Suit Shows Intervention by Merck Officials," *The New York Times*, April 24, 2005, p. 1. See also: Alex Berenson, "For Merck, the Vioxx Paper Trail Won't Go Away," *New York Times*, August 21, 2005, p. 1.

13. Testimony of David J. Graham.

14. On the Neurontin episode, see: David Callahan, *The Cheating Culture: Why More Americans Are Doing Wrong to Get Ahead* (New York: Harcourt, 2005) pp. 51–55.

CHAPTER SIX: HONORING WORK

1. See for example: Gary Langer and Jon Cohen, "Voter and Values in the 2004 Election," *Public Opinion Quarterly*, vol. 69, no. 6 (2005), pp. 744–59.

2. On being last in median income, see: "State Rankings: Median Household Income, 2003," U.S. Census Bureau, February 2006. On decline in

income, see: "Income Inequality Has Increased in West Virginia Since the Late 1970s," Center for Budget and Policy Priorities, 2002. See also: "Family Economic Security: West Virginia State Context," National Center for Children in Poverty.

3. Exit poll numbers are from CNN Election Results, 2004, West Virginia and Kentucky.

4. Quoted in Geoff Rips, "The Way of RFK," *The American Prospect*, February 12, 2001, p. 40.

5. On Bush's 2000 performance, see: Thomas B. Edsall, "Voter Values Determine Political Affiliation," *Washington Post*, March 26, 2001, p. A1.

6. Jeffrey Stonecash, *Class and Party in American Politics* (Boulder, CO: Westview Press, 2000); Larry Bartels, "What's the Matter with *What's the Matter With Kansas*," February 2006.

7. Bartels, *What's the Matter with Kansas?*, p. 10.

8. Stephen Hart, *What Does the Lord Require? How Americans Christians Think About Economic Justice* (New Brunswick, NJ: Rutgers University Press, 1996), p. xix; Wayne E. Baker and Melissa Forbes, "Moral Values and Market Attitudes," unpublished paper, April 2005.

9. David Madland, "What Would Jesus Tax: How Religion Shapes Views on Economic Policy," *Democracy and Society*, vol. 3, issue 1, Fall 2005, pp. 6–9.

10. George Lakoff, *Moral Politics: How Liberals and Conservatives Think* (Chicago: University of Chicago Press, 2002).

11. John Gaventa, *Power and Powerlessness: Quiescence & Rebellion in an Appalachian Valley* (Champaign: University of Illinois Press, 1982).

12. "Family Economic Security: Kentucky State Context," National Center for Children in Poverty; and Andrew M. Isserman, "Appalachia Then and Now: An Update of 'The Realities of Deprivation' Reported to the President in 1964," unpublished manuscript, November 1996, p. 8. On income gains, see: Economic Policy Institute/Center on Budget and Policy Priorities, "Pulling Apart: A State-by-State Analysis of Income Trends," 2002.

13. On Bush's tax cut: "Taking Stock: A Snapshot of Economic Indicators for Kentucky," Democracy Resource Center, July 17, 2004, p. 15.

14. See: Rebecca Blank, *It Takes a Nation: A New Agenda for Fighting Poverty* (Princeton, NJ: Princeton University Press, 1996).

15. "Mining Employment Trends," National Association of Mining, 2004.

16. On education, see: "West Virginia Higher Education Report Card: 2004," West Virginia Higher Education Policy Commission, 2004, p. 10; and "Measuring Up 2002," National Center for Higher Education and Public Policy, 2002.

17. For a comprehensive account of the problem, see: Beth Shulman, *The Betrayal of Work: How Low-Wage Jobs Fail 30 Million Americans and Their Families* (New York: The New Press, 2003).

18. Jane Meinhardt and Dale Brown, "SuperShuttle set to change business structure," *The Business Journal*, December 27, 2002.

19. Tamara Draut, *Strapped: Why America's Twenty- and Thirty-Somethings Can't Get Ahead* (New York: Doubleday, 2006).

20. A comprehensive guide to research and policy in this area can be found at www.assetbuilding.org, a website of the New America Foundation.

CHAPTER SEVEN: WHO CARES ABOUT THE POOR?

1. Sharon Parrott, Edwin Park, and Robert Greenstein, "Assessing the Effects of the Budget Conference Agreement on Low-income Families and Individuals," Center on Budget and Policy Priorities, December 20, 2005.

2. Mark Mellman and Sam Munger, "Using the Right Words Gets the Message to Opinion Leaders About Helping Low-income Families, National Center for Children in Poverty, Winter 2003.

3. Tom W. Smith, "Altruism and Empathy in America: Trends and Correlates," National Opinion Research Center, University of Chicago, February 6, 2006, p. 3.

4. Marvin Olasky, *Compassionate Conservatism: What It Is, What It Does, and How It Can Transform America* (New York: The Free Press, 2000), p. 4; Marvin Olasky, *The Tragedy of American Compassion* (Washington, D.C.: Regnery Publishing, Inc., 1992), p. 214.

5. Olasky, *Compassionate Conservatism*, p. 14.

6. Olasky, *The Tragedy of American Compassion*, p. 232.

7. Martin Seligman, *Authentic Happiness: Using the New Positive Psychology to Realize Your Potential for Lasting Fulfillment* (New York: Free Press, 2002).

8. Dorothy Rosenbaum and Zoe Neuberger, "Food and Nutrition Programs: Reducing Hunger, Bolstering Nutrition," Center on Budget and Policy Priorities, July 19, 2005, p. 7.

9. "Poverty Status of Families by Type of Family Presence of Related Children, Race, Hispanic Origin: 1959 to 2004," U.S. Census Bureau, 2005; James Johnson, Jr., "The Changing Face of Poverty in North Carolina," *Popular Government*, Spring/Summer 2003, p., 17.

10. "The 2005 North Carolina Living Income Standard," North Carolina Justice Center.

11. Johnson, "The Changing Face of Poverty in North Carolina," pp. 14–24; Sorien K. Schmidt, "Poverty and the Economy in North Carolina," North Carolina Justice Center, November 18, 2004, p. 16.

12. "Charitable Giving Rises 5 Percent to Nearly $250 Billion in 2004," Giving USA Foundation, 2005.

13. Eileen P. Sweeney and Shawn Fremstad, "Supplemental Security Income: Supporting People with Disabilities and the Elderly Poor," Center for Budget and Policy Priorities, August 17, 2005.

14. Ann O'Hara and Emily Cooper, "Priced Out in 2004: The Housing Crisis for People with Disabilities," Technical Assistance Collaborative/Consortium for Citizens with Disabilities Housing Task Force, August 2005, p. 42.

15. Ibid., p. 5.

Chapter Eight: The Meaning of Patriotism

1. Tim Layden, "A Star NFL Player Leaves the Game to Serve His Country," *Sports Illustrated*, June 3, 2002.

2. Hal Habib, "Destination Canton," *Palm Beach Post*, July 17, 2005.

3. "Ex-NFL Star Tillman Makes 'Ultimate Sacrifice': Safety, Who Gave Up Big Salary To Join Army, Killed in Afghanistan," MSNBC, April 26, 2004.

4. Marco R. della Cava, "Tillman memorialized in hometown," *USA Today*, May 3, 2004.

5. Tillman's parents quoted in: "Tillman's family critical of way Army handled his death," *USA Today*, May 23, 2005; and Frank Rich, "The Mysterious Death of Pat Tillman," *New York Times*, November 6, 2005.

6. George Orwell, "Notes On Nationalism," 1945; *Polls on Patriotism and Military Service* (Washington, D.C.: American Enterprise Institute, 2005), pp. 7–9, 28; "Wave of Post-September 11th Patriotism Falls Flat," Harwood Institute/Gallup Poll, Feburary 18, 2002; *Polls on Patriotism and Military Service*, p. 28. For additional discussions of patriotism, see: Daniel Bar-Tal and Ewing Staub, eds., *Patriotism* (Chicago: Nelson-Hall, 1997); Christopher S. Parker, "Shades of Patriotism: Group Identity, National Identity, and Democracy," unpublished paper.

7. Todd Gitlin, *The Intellectuals and the Flag* (New York: Columbia University Press, 2005), p. 139.

8. "America's Neglected Veterans," Harvard/Cambridge Hospital Study Group, October 19, 2004.

9. "Snapshot of How VA Budget Shortfall Is Hurting Veterans' Access to Safe and Timely Care Across the Nation," House Committee on Veterans, June 29, 2005.

10. Charles Hoge et al., "Combat Duty in Iraq and Afghanistan: Mental Health Problems, and Barriers to Care," *New England Journal of Medicine*, July 2004, pp. 13–22.

11. "Effects of the Bush Tax Cuts Enacted through 2004 (with sunsets) by Income Group," Center for Tax Justice, July 2005.

12. "List of Corporate Tax Dodgers," Citizen Works, 2003.

13. "25 Fortune 500 Corporations with the Most Offshore Tax-Haven Subsidiaries," Citizen Works, 2003.

14. Charlie Cray and Lee Drutman, "Sacrifice Is For Suckers: How Corporations Are Using Offshore Tax Havens to Avoid Paying Taxes," Citizen Works, 2003.

15. David Cay Johnston, "U.S. Corporations Are Using Bermuda to Slash Tax Bills," *New York Times*, February 18, 2002.

16. Dan Ackman, "Stanley Works Stays Home," *Forbes.com*, August 2, 2002.

17. Jim McTague, "Tax Havens Make Senators See Red, White and Blue," *Barron's*, April 22, 2002; see also: "O'Neill Urges Tax Fix to Stem Off-shores," *Reuters*, May 17, 2002.

18. Laura Incalcaterra, "Honoring Sacrifice," *The Journal News*, January 13, 2005.

19. Neil Howe and William Strauss, *Millennials Rising: The Next Great Generation* (New York: Vintage, 2000), chapter 1.

index